People Cities

Annie Matan and Peter Newman

People Cities

The Life and Legacy of Jan Gehl

ISLANDPRESS
Washington | Covelo | London

With thanks to -
Jan and Ingrid Gehl
Realdania Foundation

Those that have added their stories to this book (in order of appearance in this book): Enrique Peñalosa, Camilla Richter-Friis van Deurs, Klaus Bondam, Rob Adams, Clover Moore, Janette Sadik-Khan, Toshio Kitahara, Brett Wood Gush, and Tom Nielsen.
Those that have helped us and assisted in the development of the book – Gehl Architects, Jan Newman, Jean-Paul Horrè, Christine Finlay, Pilar Kasat, City of Perth.

Project team
Editor: Heather Boyer, Island Press
Publisher of Danish edition: Kim Dirckinck-Holmfeld, BOGVÆRKET
Advice and guidance, fact checking, images, and historical information: Birgitte Bundesen Svarre, Gehl Architects
Graphics and images: Lars Gemzøe, Gehl Architects
Layout: Margrethe Mokrzycki, Mokrzycki Grafisk Design

Island Press is a trademark of The Center for Resource Economics.

Library of Congress Control Number: 2016947848

Printed on recycled, acid-free paper

Manufactured in the United States of America
10 9 8 7 6 5 4 3 2 1

CONTENTS

FOREWORD

by Enrique Peñalosa, Mayor of Bogotá, Colombia, 1998–2001, re-elected in 2015

When I became mayor of Bogotá in 1998, I was obsessed with getting cars off sidewalks and creating a network of hundreds of kilometers of protected bikeways. It was painfully difficult. Cars had been parking on sidewalks, or where there should have been sidewalks, for decades. There was not one block in the city where somebody on a wheelchair could go from one corner to the other on a sidewalk.

Talking about bikeways was even more difficult. At that time, there were no major bikeways in any city in America, not even in European cities such as Paris or Madrid.

But, of course, we knew of Dutch cities and of Copenhagen. We had some support from a Dutch NGO for our project to create a safer urban environment for everyone in Bogotá. And as soon as I could, I visited Copenhagen to see its bicycle and pedestrian infrastructure for myself.

Once in Copenhagen, I asked some urbanists "what book about urban planning, with emphasis on pedestrian space and bicycling, could I buy?" "What urbanist could I meet?" They recommended Jan Gehl and his book: *Life Between Buildings.*

I was fascinated by the book. My intuition and vision now had a backbone. Then something marvelous happened: Jan's daughter moved to Bogotá to work for an NGO. This made Jan travel, not once but several times, to Bogotá. We took him on our recently built bikeway network and on our greenways, and we made several presentations.

I discovered, beyond urban matters, what a marvelous human being Jan is, to everybody, what a great sense of humor he has, and even what a fun musician he is with the group of friends with whom he plays the trombone. It is evident that his work on humane cities stems from the way he lives and enjoys life: above all, he wants to make cities that are happier cities, more-fun places to live in.

Jan and I became friends. We met in many places, and I was one of many promoting his gospel all over the world.

Beyond his direct advisory work, Jan has influenced hundreds of cities all over the world to become more humane and happier. I am thankful to know Jan, learn from him, and enjoy him as a human being.

Jan Gehl and Enrique Peñalosa testing the new bicycle infrastructure in Bogotá in November 2003. The bicycle rickshaw was brought along by the good host because Jan was suffering from a knee injury.

PREFACE

ANNIE'S STORY

In 2007, I had just returned to Perth after studying and working in the US for six years. I was very interested in continuing my research in walkability and urban design, particularly how people relate to the built environment and why we are continually creating places that people do not like. Through my studies, I had been introduced to Jan Gehl's work, and undertook a Jan-Gehl-type Public Space Public Life survey of the city center in Fremantle, Western Australia. This study fueled my desire to undertake more. I was lucky enough to have Jan review this study and then, when he visited Perth in early 2008, to have Peter Newman introduce me to Jan. Jan mentioned that he could use some assistance for the book from Birgitte Svarre on methodologies to study public life.

Before I knew it, I was on a plane to Copenhagen, where I spent over three months working with Jan and Birgitte and others at Gehl Architects. I was also living in a city where public space and people's enjoyment of space is put first in planning. It was a life-changing experience.

Returning to Perth, on my journey home from the airport, I kept thinking that everything was moving too fast, and then I realized that it had been the first time in three months that I had been in a car. The world was rushing by. In 2008, while in Copenhagen, and also back in Perth, I worked with Jan, Anna Modin, and their team from Gehl Architects on the second Perth Public Space Public Life survey, carried out 15 years after the earlier study. I worked on planning the survey and then helping coordinate the undertaking of the surveys with the City of Perth, the Department of Planning and Infrastructure, and Curtin University (with Murdoch University). Spending many hours watching how a city street works is certainly an eye-opening experience. Observing Jan's insights first-hand is also eye opening.

The survey was launched in 2009, and Jan returned to Perth with heavy media attention and a number of big public events, all of which he handled with his grace and good humor. This work set up the next decade of change in our city. The city today is a dramatically different place in terms of street life. Everyone who knew the city center 10 or 20 years ago will readily agree that the new central Perth is a far better place. But very few people know how important Jan's role was in this transformation.

This book highlights Jan's role in humanizing cities around the world, which had its non-European debut in Perth.

PETER'S STORY

I am from Perth, a city not known for any great contribution to urban design theory or practice, though it has a long tradition of commitment to planning in the modernist paradigm. Perth was the city that was first in the English-speaking world to ask Jan Gehl to come and help us revive our city center. This is how it happened.

In 1976, I was elected to the Fremantle City Council, a historic part of the Perth Metropolitan Region with one of the most intact examples of nineteenth-century Victorian and Georgian port city architecture. Our group took over the council with a set of principles that would respect the buildings, the streets, indeed the whole fabric of this old walking city. We felt our way toward this future and eventually won as developers, traders, business leaders, and the professional staff began to see that this was indeed a better way to go, and this could work.

On this journey, which I later realized was part of a movement to deconstruct modernist town planning, we had only a few experts to guide us. Jan Gehl was one.

In 1977, I read Jan's booklet from Melbourne, "The Interface Between Public and Private Territories in Residential Areas," published the year before. It is a study of some Australian suburban streets and the importance of the semi-public areas between the street and the front door of a house. Jan had watched how this semi-public area was used to increase neighborliness, in contrast to the modernist suburb that set back the house so far that people in the front of their house could no longer relate to someone walking past but merely drive into their garage and disappear inside. He also criticized older suburbs for allowing big brick fences to be built as a sound wall and to increase privacy for people in small homes. Fremantle Council had begun to allow these big walls, so I introduced a motion in the council that front fences be no more than the height that an adult could lean on, as suggested by Jan. The regulation was passed and continues today.

What impressed me most about Jan's booklet was that he had determined a policy by just watching how people used a space and that the principles he was looking to enable for the city were fundamentally good. He wanted to respect the old fabric for what it did well—bring people together and create an equitable and environmentally sensible use of space. I was emboldened as a City Councilor and, eventually, as an academic trying to find a more sustainable city.

The 1993 Perth team: academics, city and state planners, City Vision activists, and students ready for field work.

In 1991, I was asked by the state government to run a conference with an NGO called City Vision on how to imagine a better Perth. We had been implementing the modernist Stephenson Hepburn Plan for 40 years, and things were not working. The city had sprawled dramatically with low-density housing, large setbacks, and wide, high-capacity roads. The freeways and highways were highly congested, the public transport was failing, and the Perth city center was almost abandoned as a place to visit or to live in. The only success stories were the regeneration of Fremantle and the return of the railways. Since I had some involvement in both of these successes, I was asked to put together a group of people from around the world who could help us do some thinking about our urban future.

One of the first people I invited was Jan. He did not have an international reputation at this time, but based on his booklet, I wrote to him about our challenges, and he agreed to come to Perth for the conference. The City Challenge conference in September 1992 was a dramatic success. A packed house listened intently to Robert Cervero (from Berkeley), Art Eggleton (former Mayor from Toronto), Barrow Emerson (from Portland), and locals like Janet Holmes á Court and myself. But most importantly, they listened to Jan. With a delightful accent, Jan told humorous stories about what was wrong with our city and most others around the world that had lost the human element in their planning and design. With amazing slides, he showed us that Copenhagen had similarly given up its city to the car but now was fighting back and slowly beginning to win.

In the audience, I turned to Jim, my policy assistant from the Department of the Premier and Cabinet, and we both agreed—we need to bring Jan Gehl to Perth to do more detailed work. And so it happened in the Australian summer of 1992 moving into 1993 that Jan and Ingrid Gehl came to Perth for six weeks. With an extraordinarily devoted group of students, we did a detailed Public Space Public Life survey in Central Perth.

Other cities in Australia soon followed and the Gehl train left the station to take on some of the big cities of the world.

Opposite: Responding to the 1993 Perth study. Perth Cultural Centre in 1993 (top) and 2015 (bottom). Introducing the people-scale to the modernist cultural buildings has completely turned the place around.

1

THE HUMAN DIMENSION

THE HUMAN DIMENSION

"If Jan Gehl did not already exist, it would be necessary to invent him to rescue our cities. At the center of the urban universe are a city's people, and for a half-century, Jan's visionary work has helped cities adapt their public space to their people instead of to their traffic. Jan's is that rare mix of sensitivity, intelligence and humor to detect the essential problems of urban design and devise the practical, city-specific solutions needed to overcome them."

—Janette Sadik-Khan, Bloomberg Associates; Commissioner, New York City Department of Transportation, 2007-2013; author, *Streetfight: Handbook for an Urban Revolution*

While others have called for a more humane approach to cities over the years, no one has had the influence in shaping cities and changing the way that we think about urban design as Jan Gehl. Much has been written by Jan about his approach, and by others about his influence, but this book tells the inside story of how he learned to study urban spaces and implement his people-centered approach to architecture and urban design. It is the human side of the story. *People Cities* discusses the work, theory, life, and influence of Jan Gehl from our perspective of working with Jan in our home city of Perth, as well as in Copenhagen, and includes stories from others who have worked with him in cities across the globe.

Working with Jan, we found that he could not only explain what was wrong with cities, but more importantly, how they should be fixed. He provided the tools necessary to put the human back in the center of planning, design, and architecture.

We take an approach that combines biography and the development of his research and practice-based methodology, with stories of his influence, celebrating a change from an abstract, ideological, modernist approach to planning and architecture to an approach that considers humans. The book is organized around this important shift in planning and is structured around key periods in Jan's working life. Throughout the book, we reflect on Jan's role in developing and advancing the movement of people-oriented architecture and planning.

Jan's research and strategies have been critical in reorienting urban planning and architecture and reclaiming cities for people after modernist building principles and the great car invasion reshaped most cities after WWII. Today, as rapid urbanization continues around the globe, Jan's ideas are even more important in assuring that a growing number of people have inviting, comfortable, safe urban environments.

The global urban population is expected to reach 66 percent of the entire global population by 2050. It is a critical time to examine how we can all become advocates for a people-centered approach to architecture and planning within our cities. It is also a fitting time to reflect on the power of Jan Gehl's life and work as he turns 80 in 2016.

Jan has been studying and applying his ideas for improving public space for over 50 years in cities around the world—first through his academic career and then through the work of his firm, Gehl Architects. His work has had a distinct influence on how urban designers and architects make projects, and it has been applied to some of the world's most high-profile cities, including New York, London, Mos-

> *I am an architect, educated as an architect. I graduated in 1960 in the days of modernism when city was bad and…putting buildings freely on grass was good…Architects were towering over the projects, and sort of making compositions. That was my training…*
>
> —Jan Gehl, October 2008

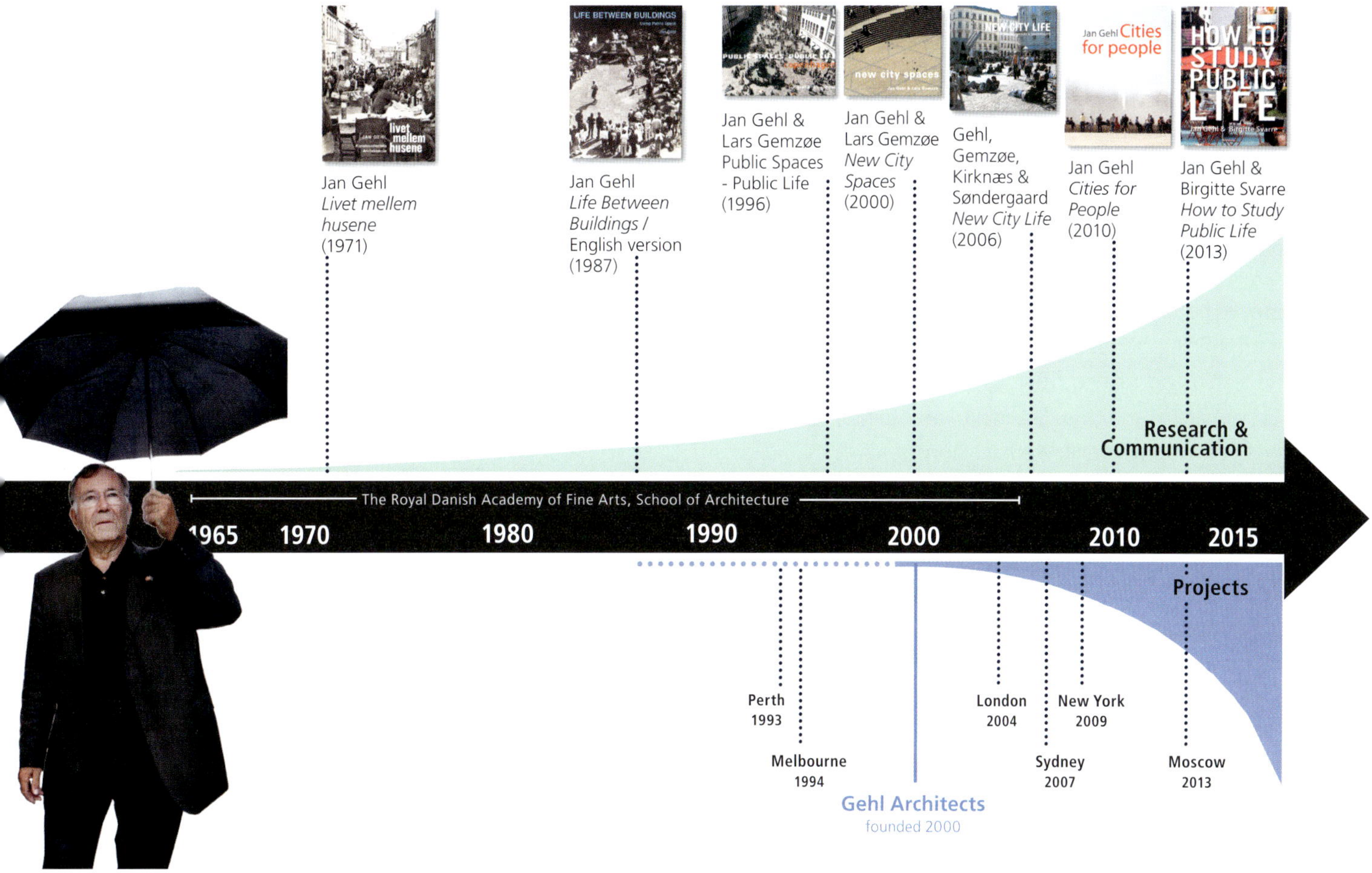

cow, Copenhagen, Melbourne, and Sydney—as well as our own city of Perth.

As a theorist, Jan is explicitly humanist and pro-urban, always emphasizing that we must design "cities for people", rather than purely for vehicle movement, architectural flourish, or blind, simplistic economics. He believes that good architecture is not just about form, but about the interaction between form and life. The design of cities should maximize the diversity of social exchange while minimizing travel needs, enabling people to enjoy life in public spaces, creating chances for people to meet accidentally and intentionally, continually bringing people to the forefront. Jan sees neighborhoods and cities as places for human opportunity. Design must be about how this opportunity is facilitated. This approach to design grew in parallel with the theories of other urban experts, including Jane Jacobs, William "Holly" Whyte, and Donald Appleyard. Jan has become perhaps the most well-known proponent for this approach due to his global work, his persistence, and his considerable communication skills.

Jan considers his work to have three major phases: (1) research and theory development, starting from the 1960s; (2) the development and testing of his methodology in real-life projects, starting in Copenhagen in the late 1960s; and (3) communication and expansion of his methods and ideas by publishing his books worldwide as well as working on projects in cities across the globe (1990s onward).

Throughout his career, Jan has battled to "make people visible" within architecture and city planning. He is not satisfied to simply have his ideas adopted, but has worked to implement them. He has consistently tested and developed his theory in an iterative process: proposing theory, testing it in practice, and then refining his ideas. The next city in which he tested and refined these approaches, after Copenhagen and the Scandinavian capitals, was Perth. So we begin with our story of Jan in Perth; a story that is continued later in the book

Note on modernism

Modernism is a technocratic approach based on the idea of the city as a machine that arose as a response to the social and economic confusion and disillusionment created by industrial cities, the depression of the 1890s, and the collapse of many certainties in the horrors of World War I.

PERTH, WESTERN AUSTRALIA: THE PERFECT MODERNIST CITY

Perth, the capital city of Western Australia, was seen by Jan in 1992 as an unrivalled example of a modernist city and of "motorist planning."[1] The city was perfectly structured around separated land use—with work here, shop there, sleep elsewhere—and around accommodating the car. Signs throughout the city center said "your car's as welcome as you are."

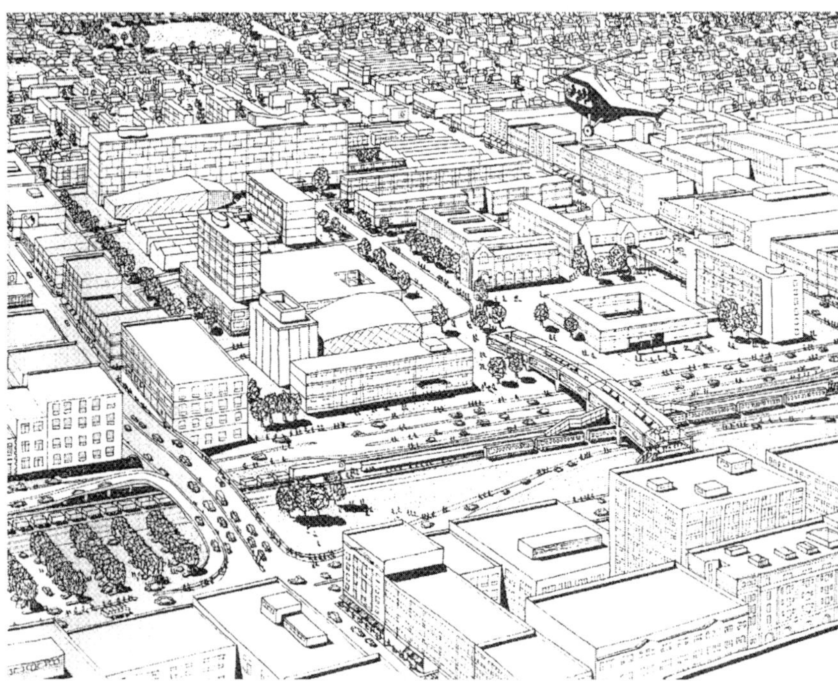

Perth, the perfect modernist city. The sketch, by Gordon Stephenson and J. A. Hepburn, shows suggested redevelopment in the Perth's city center in 1955. Your car's as welcome as you are!

Modernist cities were about the buildings and the roads, not about people and places. The belief of modernists was that this approach would make the city efficient and healthy for people since they needed fresh air, light, space, and room for cars in order to function properly. Modernism, however, overlooked the social dimension of cities and architecture—that people also want to experience other people, life, vitality, and diversity.

Despite the criticism of modernism and the separation of land uses, particularly in North America and Australia, modernism was established within global planning as the dominant doctrine. Various professions began to organize, plan, and describe cities as a series of separate functions rather than a complex system of interactions between people.

Probably the smallest for any city its size, the Perth city center was characterized as an oversized department store surrounded by parking structures. (From "Public Space Public Life in Perth, 1994")

Perth was laid out as an administrative and military hub by Septimus Roe in 1833. After an early period of villages and growth in the 1890s due to the gold rush, the city was restructured based on the modernist metropolitan plan of Gordon Stephenson and Alistair Hepburn in 1955. This was the same period in which Brasilia, the new capital of Brazil, was conceived as the perfect modernist town. The Perth plan called for an urban form based around car transport, low-density suburban sprawl, and a freeway system. The plan was commissioned by the state government in 1953 to guide development of the metropolitan region based on the idea of the modern city and the largely American ideal of the *good* city that was sweeping the world at the time.

As a result of this plan and the introduction of affordable cars, suburbanization in the area grew rapidly. People moved out of the city center into the new suburbs, and the city center became a place only for trade and work. Major road and bridge construction began, and the Swan River was partially filled in during the late 1950s to make room for freeways along the shores.

Office skyscrapers came to dominate Perth's skyline. By the 1990s, the commercial orientation of the city center meant that the streets were dominated with car traffic coming from the surrounding suburbs. People drove to the city and then drove home, creating a city that was congested during rush hours, busy during the day, and totally abandoned at night. The city recognized that it had a problem. So the

City of Perth and the Government of Western Australia in 1992 invited Jan to conduct a survey in the city center on the use of public space by people. The 1993 survey, later to be called the Public Space Public Life survey, was the first non-Scandinavian survey of this type. Jan determined that Perth was a city with "no invitation for walking, and certainly no great invitation to walk for the pleasure of walking."[2] He concluded that Perth essentially had the "character of an oversized department store" and that the two pedestrian streets were "conceived not as walking routes but as isolated islands in a car-traffic-dominated city."[3] The pedestrian streets in Perth were essentially shopping-mall corridors in which people could walk a bit, then look around and then walk back because they were not connected to any larger pedestrian network. They went from nowhere to nowhere.

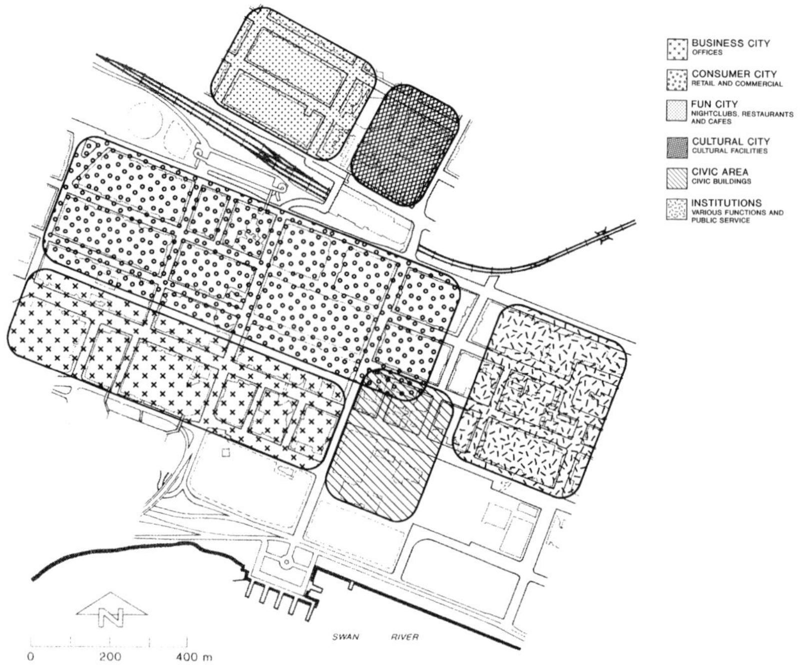

Perth, the perfect modernist city. The land use plan shows distinctly separate areas for work, shopping, and fun, with no residences in sight. (From "Public Space Public Life in Perth, 1994")

"Your car's as welcome as you are," but in reality, your car was considerably more welcome. Left: Four lanes of traffic on Murray Street (1985). Above: Wanting to cross a street? Please apply here!

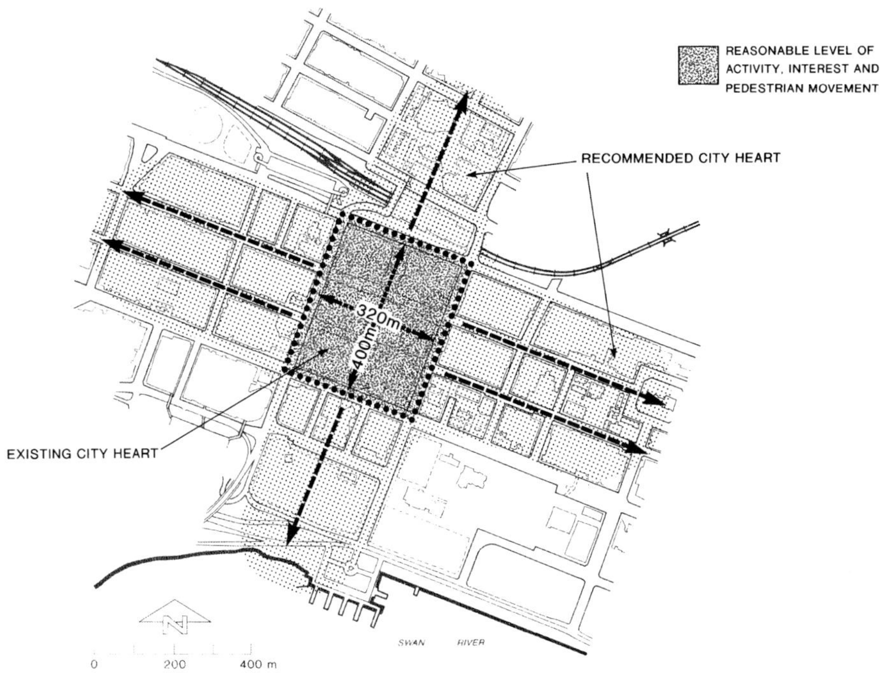

Jan's recommendations for improving the city involved expanding the city center in all four directions, all the way down to the riverbank, and turning what resembled a shopping center into a true city center. (From "Public Space Public Life in Perth, 1994")

Fundamentally, Jan's Public Space Public Life survey revealed a planning-and-design system focused purely on car movement and commercial activity—the city center was, in fact, trying to copy suburban shopping centers. Additionally, the survey highlighted that walking was not seen as public life, and that public space included only those event spaces and grand public areas where major civic events could occasionally occur, not the everyday public realm of the city.

It was a damning report. It was also a significant risk for Jan, who was hired by the city and state government, to have produced such a report instead of softening the findings to make it more acceptable. As Jan states, "Being an old Boy Scout, I always had this impractical urge to tell the truth, more or less."

The survey concluded with a number of recommendations that the city could use to transform itself into more of a people city. These included walking the city down to the river in order to take advantage of the city's natural asset, the Swan River foreshore, and expanding the city to reach right down to the attractive river shore. Jan concluded: "The heart of the city must be expanded for the sake of the city—so one really feels that the city is more than two blocks; so people moving about clearly get the signal that this is a significant city, the strong heart of a great region."[4]

According to Jan, this became one of the most memorable working periods of his life. He lived and worked in the city for six weeks, getting to know it and its people. The extraordinary level of enthusiasm he experienced from the group of volunteers and the city staff enhanced his experience. From here on, Jan was invited to one city after another around the world to help them become more people-oriented.

So who is Jan Gehl?

LUSTRE BAR
COFFEE
SPECIAL
Reg $3.00
Large $3.50
No extra charge

2

MAKING PEOPLE VISIBLE

MAKING PEOPLE VISIBLE

"It is interesting that so much is known about good habitats for mountain gorillas and Siberian tigers, while, at the same time, only very little is known about a good urban habitat for Homo sapiens."
—Enrique Peñalosa, Mayor of Bogotá, Colombia

Jan Gehl was born in Rønne, a provincial town in Denmark on September 17, 1936. The family moved to Copenhagen some years later, and it was there that Jan spent his boyhood, went to school, and later carried out his research. Everything was "quite ordinary" except for the fact that Jan was pushed one year forward in the school system and spent his entire education being one year younger than his schoolmates. He describes his home as full of laughter and very open, providing him with a "very stable base."

Jan initially was going to study engineering, and it wasn't until just before graduating high school that he became aware of the possibility of studying architecture, which sounded much more diverse and exciting to him than engineering. There were no architectural traditions in his family—no architect relatives or other sources of inspiration. It was unknown territory.

According to Jan, his was a rather ordinary, middle-class family, the father working in a government office position and his mother at home caring for the children. His mother had a strong interest in history and his father in building, constantly working on their summer home. Much later in life, Jan discovered that his father had always wanted to be an architect, so he must have influenced Jan somehow.

Jan became the first member of his family to obtain a university education and, in 1960, at 23 years of age, he graduated with a master's degree from the School of Architecture at the Royal Danish Academy of Fine Arts in Copenhagen.

In 1961, Jan married Ingrid Mundt (now Gehl), a student of psychology, who would shortly join that profession. As the story goes, that Ingrid and the other friends of the young family who were psychologists, sociologists, doctors, or the like started to ask Jan and his architecture friends "Why are you architects not interested in people?" "Why don't they teach you anything about people in architecture schools?" "What do you think about the fact that your architecture professors take their photos at four o'clock in the morning to ensure that the architecture can be enjoyed without the distraction of people in the photos?" Altogether, these made for a disturbing "bucket of questions" for a young architect trained to practice modernism. Ingrid's work in psychology came to very strongly influence Jan's approach to architecture and urban design, prompting a focus on how people relate to the built environment. The 1960s, in general, was a time of radical rethinking and questioning of the establishment and the established orders. It was a time of intense

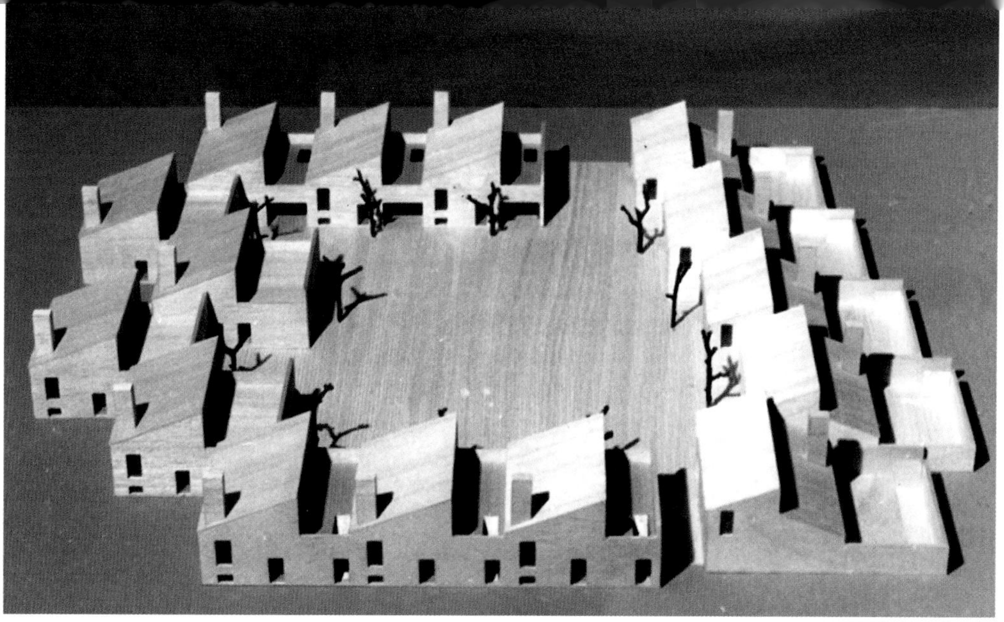

The Amtsstuegården residential project, 1962–63. The houses were gathered in little clusters around a common square. Eleven such clusters made up the project.

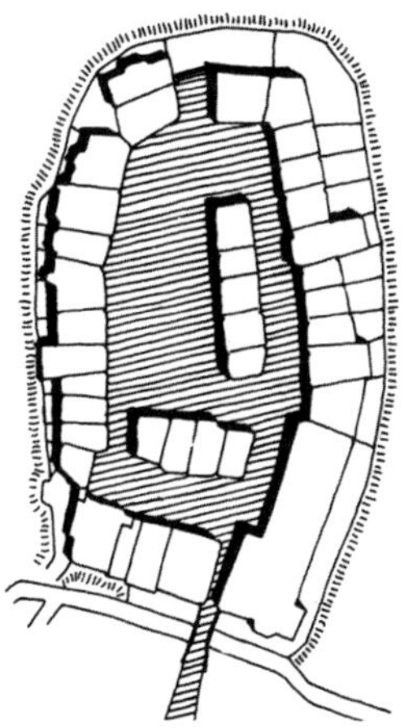

The architects were inspired by small Italian villages such as San Vittorino Romano (left). The newspaper cartoon shows the architect explaining how "la dolce vita" can unfold in the Danish suburbs. The project was never realized because it was too bold.

public debate about who knows what is best for citizens. In some cities, such as Copenhagen, the debate focused on the changes happening to the city. Jan was part of this debate.

Looking around at his profession in Copenhagen, Jan became "incensed by the way the built environment and modern city planning were treating people in new housing, in new city districts, and in the existing city neighborhoods." The new modernist housing block areas were devoid of human life, and the suburban areas became places only for sleeping. The human aspects were completely overlooked.

After graduation, Jan worked for two years for architects Viggo Møller-Jensen and Tyge Arnfred. During this period, he worked on a number of residential projects, foremost a rather big social-housing project in Godthaab (now named Nuuk), the capital of Greenland. Møller-Jensen and Arnfred had an outstanding reputation as solid humanists and among the best housing architects in Denmark—not a bad place for a young architect to start his career.

In 1962, after a brief period of forced military service, Jan began working in the office of architect couple Inger and Johannes Exner in Copenhagen. They focused mainly on restoration work and the design and construction of churches. Here, Jan worked primarily on restoring medieval churches, work which

Measuring colonial buildings in Greenland, 1959

The School of Architecture in Copenhagen had a strong tradition of developing skills for measuring. Jan was an eager participant, and spurred by his interest in history, engaged in extra courses centered on measuring and studying old medieval churches, mostly in rural villages. With this background, Jan took part in a four-month-long expedition to Greenland in the summer and fall of 1959. The purpose was to measure and record the old Danish colonial buildings. The project was organized by the Danish National Museum.

Measuring sacred ruins in Greece, 1963

In the summer of 1963, Jan and nine other architects and students from the Copenhagen School of Architecture spent four months in Delphi, Greece with the task of making an unprecedented measurement of the entire sanctuary in Delphi. While the oracle was not found, an impressive, very precise plan of the archaeological site was produced. Strangely, a precise recording of the sanctuary had not been done previously. The search for treasures and sculptures had dominated the mindsets of earlier excavators. One early plan even had the number of temple columns wrong! The project was organized by the French Archaeological School in Athens.

The restoration of the traditional village church on the island of Sejerø (1964–67) became the first independent work by Jan as an architect. Since 1950, the Gehl family has spent their summers in a cottage on this island. Left: Exterior view, watercolor by Jan. Above: Work on repairing the tower in progress.

ranged from archeological digs to work on both the exteriors and the interiors, including designing lamps, altars, and organs. This is something he continued for quite a few years, restoring churches as a "discrete sideshow" to his later academic work. He was very fond of this type of work, which involved the traditional crafts and close collaboration with clergymen, archeologists, and artists. It was only in the 1990s that he had to give up this sideline, as his urban design work became more and more demanding. This sideline resulted in Jan restoring some twelve Danish village churches from the eleventh or twelfth century between 1962 and 1990.

It was during this period, working for Exner that Jan became involved in designing a housing development on a large piece of land near the Danish town of Hillerød. The site was being rezoned from rural to urban, and the very idealistic landowner wanted to leave a legacy. He asked very specifically for a housing area that was "good for people," not the usual scattering of suburban houses or "concrete blocks of flats."

This presented quite a challenge for the architects in the office: "good for people, what was that?" It was an unheard-of challenge in the early 1960s, and they struggled with what to do.

New ways of thinking were required. In order to do this, the architects consulted with a sociologist. This was very likely the first time that a sociologist was involved in a housing design project in Denmark. The question of how to make housing good for people was at this time a new and thought-provoking question. It soon appeared that the sociologist involved did not know much either. The experience opened Jan's eyes to the impor-

Sembra ma non è un «beatnik»

Da diversi giorni abbiamo notato un giovane straniero aggirarsi per la Piazza del Popolo. Abbiamo subito pensato: «I beatnick» in Ascoli?

Ma il suo fare aveva qualcosa di particolare. A parte le misurazioni ed i rilievi con strani apparecchi ottici, lo straniero prendeva in continuazione appunti su tutti i passanti. Insomma chi era?

Poche parole di presentazione e di saluto e subito si è scoperto l'arcano. Si tratta dell'architetto danese Jan Gehl, che avendo ricevuto una borsa di studio per studiare la forma e la vita delle piazze italiane da un punto di vista architettonico e sociologico, ha incluso la nostra Piazza del Popolo nei suoi itinerari.

Il giovane e simpaticissimo architetto, che si avvale della collaborazione della gentile consorte laureata in psicologia, si va chiedendo perché mai — nei centri storici italiani — con tanti viali e belle strade nuove, la popolazione insista a passeggiare sulle antiche piazze.

Saremmo interessati, al termine delle sue indagini, di conoscere se ha svelato l'arcano del nostro inguaribile «passeggiar piazza». (Foto Riga)

Measuring people in Italy, 1965

Above: "He looks like a beatnik but he is not" from a newspaper in Ascoli Piceno, Italy, fall 1965. The journalist was obviously puzzled by the peculiar behavior of a "people student."

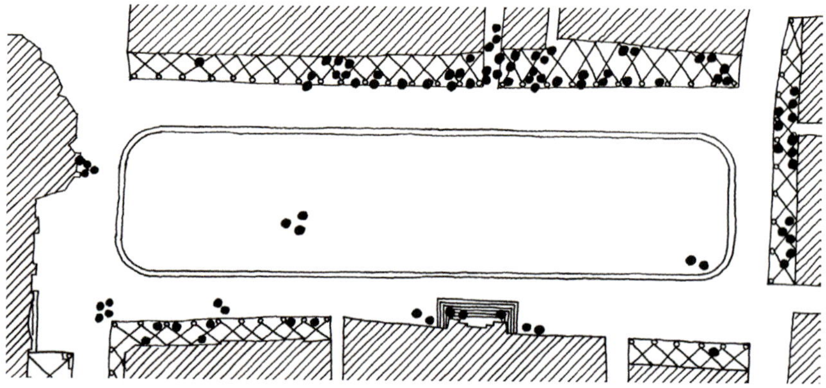

Top: Study from the city square in Ascoli Piceno showing where all the people not walking in the square were gathered. Clearly, the edges and the niches were favored by the people spending time in the square.

tance of bringing together social science and architecture to develop new insights.

The resulting plan for the housing development, Amtsstuegården, was a series of low-rise residencies clustered around common, shared public spaces. The shared squares were the core of the proposal. The proposal was widely published, debated, and referenced in Denmark. However, the project was never built as it was considered too avant-garde for Denmark at the time. The idea of sharing squares with neighbors in order to facilitate social contact was considered too risky in a rather conservative housing market.

However, things were starting to change in Copenhagen. In 1962, the city council converted its one-kilometer-long main street, known as Strøget, into a pedestrian street. It started as a temporary experiment, but was soon made permanent. It has frequently been assumed that Jan was involved somehow in the permanent closing of Strøget to vehicles. However, this was not the case. He studied Strøget, starting some years after the conversion, and later, through his studies, came to influence further developments within Copenhagen (discussed later in the book). The initial closing of Strøget in 1962 was, in many ways, a pioneering project, one of the earliest in Europe, but certainly not the first. Several Danish provincial cities such as Randers, Aalborg, and Holstebro had also pedestrianized their main streets around this time. The main idea behind closing Strøget to traffic was to provide a pleasant shopping and business district to compete with the new enclosed shopping malls that were being built in the suburbs. The experiment was much debated, with critics asserting that "we are Danes, not Italians"

Jan's studies of where people choose to stay in public spaces quickly led to identifying the importance of "supports for staying." If the bollards in the Campo in Siena were removed, most life in the square would diminish.

and that "Danes would never *promenade* on the streets or sit in the squares in Copenhagen." Such behavior was not suited for the northern mentality and would actually be impossible due to the Nordic climate. However, the car-free street was an immediate success, with pedestrian numbers increasing dramatically in the first year.

The Amtsstuegården housing proposal was Jan's first involvement in researching and designing with an emphasis on the public realm. He refers to it as the first project he was able to work on with values. This project—and the emphasis on the spaces between the buildings being particularly "good for people"—had a huge impact on Jan's work. The inspiration, combined with curiosity, led Jan and Ingrid to set out for Italy in 1965 to try to find out something essential about how people use public spaces. They believed that "if anything at all could be found about people in cities, it had to be in Italy."

LIFE IN THE ITALIAN PIAZZAS: 1965

For six months in the fall of 1965, Jan and Ingrid, supported by a Rome Scholarship from The New Carlsberg Foundation, travelled in Italy and studied the use of public spaces and everyday public life in the cities of Lucca, Ascoli Piceno, Martina Franca, and Rome. Jan and Ingrid were: "drawn in by the human activity they saw between and in cities and towns that had not yet been reorganized by rational planners or invaded by cars."[5] According to Jan and Ingrid, the "public space in Italy's old cities seethed with life."[6]

Jan and Ingrid were fascinated by the human ecosystem and the diversity of activities in these Italian cities. They became engrossed in studying the intricate details of

A collage of clippings from Danish newspapers and magazines from the 1960s showing the public interest in this intriguing combination of a psychologist and an architect talking about the quality of the physical environment. One headline reads, "Hurrah for the Gehls." Another, written by an elderly journalist, suggests that money spent on studying public life is money wasted: "Public life is so obvious and well known that there is surely no need to know more!"

A film clip of Jan and Ingrid in 1967 explaining the virtues of pedestrianizing city streets. This was recently shown on Danish national television in a series exploring Denmark's history.

daily life in the urban spaces, to learn what worked and what did not work in terms of urban design.

In Italy, Jan became particularly interested in investigating why and where people chose to sit, stand, and socialize within public spaces. In the Piazza del Popolo, Ascoli Piceno, he and Ingrid started dividing people's activities in public spaces into categories such as *necessary* and *optional*—two activity categories with very different demands on the physical environment. They tested different ways of recording and mapping the activities of people. Jan and Ingrid started to observe how and why places were working for people by recording specific details, including the number of people sitting and standing in various locations and the number of pedestrians on various streets. The importance of the edges of public space became quite clear, with people clustering along them in the piazzas to rest and watch the daily activities. This use of edges fascinated Jan and is a theme he returns to again and again.

After their immersion in the Italian streetscapes, the couple published the results of their studies in a series of articles in *Arkitekten*, the Danish architectural journal, in early 1966.[7] The articles were considered rather exceptional at the time because it was a novelty to include detailed studies of human behavior in an architectural context.

The Italian studies laid the foundation for the rest of Jan's work, both in theory and in research methodology. In Italy, and then later at the Royal Danish Academy of Fine Arts, he continually developed the methods and tested findings. The understanding of the different uses of space and the role of design started to become apparent.

BEYOND CRITIQUING MODERNIST PLANNING

Their work in Italy gave Ingrid and Jan a reputation as public academics and even activists. They began to rise to prominence in Denmark for questioning and criticizing both the widespread areas of single-family housing and the modernist housing projects that were being built. Together, they published numerous articles challenging the arrogance of some of

Høje Gladsaxe, a low-cost housing project with five 13-story residential blocks surrounded by a very formalistic landscape. In 1969, 50 students from the Sociologists, Psychologists and Architects study group, and 50 incensed parents from the housing project joined forces and created a brand new playground to overcome the rigid landscaping. The Høje Gladsaxe architects called it "an act of vandalism against the architecture." The Danish Institute of Architects assisted with part of the funding for the protest project. It was a time of great contrasts!

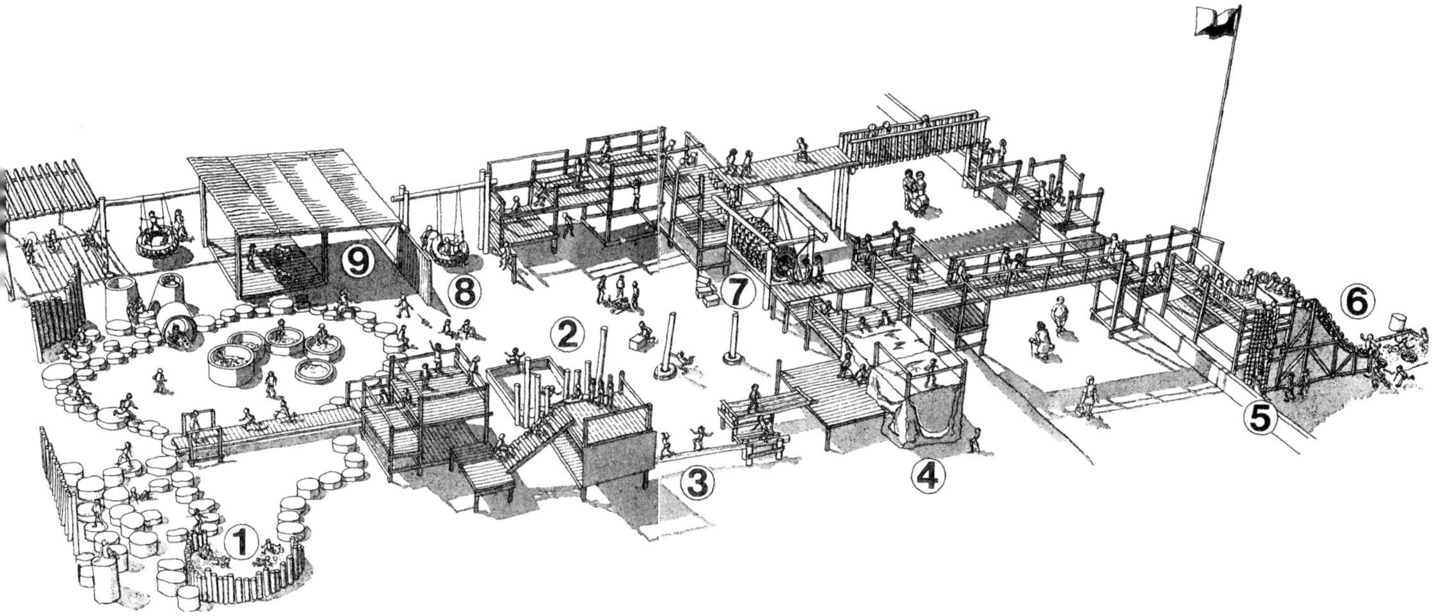

This drawing shows Høje Gladsaxe's new play landscape. Artists, architects, designers, teachers, and parents joined forces to create a play landscape for all age groups. A major goal was to secure several bridges over the long wall separating the residences from the surrounding landscape. (Illustration from Bo Bedre, 10, 1969)

the architects and planners dominant in this period, particularly their lack of attention to the human scale and human needs.

Simply commenting on these issues, however, was not enough for Jan and Ingrid. It became obvious to them that architects and planners needed to have better knowledge of how people interact with the built environment. They believed that new tools were needed to study and amass basic knowledge about the interaction between people and cities. Ingrid went on to study residential issues while Jan stayed focused on life in cities from his new base at the School of Architecture in Copenhagen.

RETURNING TO THE SCHOOL OF ARCHITECTURE

In 1966, the School of Architecture at The Royal Danish Academy of Fine Arts changed status from an art school to a university, which meant that research would now be included in the tasks to be performed by the departments within the architecture school. Professor of landscape architecture, Sven-Ingvar Andersson, who had come to know Jan when he was the landscape architect for the Amtsstuegården project, invited Jan to join the school to develop his studies on the use of public space. Jan joined the landscape architecture department in a four-year research position with a focus on people's use of outdoor space in cities and residential neighborhoods.

Since Jan was part of the first generation of researchers at the school of architecture, he had a great deal of freedom to explore methods and ideas, but also a fair amount of loneliness and insecurity due to a lack of guidance, support from fellow researchers, or a research tradition. Around this time, Ingrid started working at the Danish Building Research Institute as the first environmental psychologist in Denmark, with a focus on the psychological aspect of housing. They continued working together, and her influence on Jan's work has continued throughout his career.

During this time, Jan initiated an interdisciplinary group of academics and students called SPAS (Sociologists, Psychologists, and

The vibrant Danish debate on quality of housing and books such as Living Environment *by Ingrid Gehl and* Life Between Buildings *by Jan Gehl have had a profound influence on many Danish residential projects since the 1970s.*

A morning chat across the soft edges. Solbjerg Have, Fællestegnestuen, 1977–80.

A carefully planned interface between public and private in Sibeliusparken, Fællestegnestuen, 1984–86.

Among many projects claiming to be directly influenced by Jan and Ingrid's work was the Sjølund residential project, built in 1978 and designed by architects Bente Aude and Boje Lundgaard.

Among international examples of projects inspired by the Danish research on people-oriented planning is Bo01 in Malmö, Sweden. There is a direct link between this project and the groundbreaking projects by Ralph Erskine in the 1970s and 1980s. The coordinator and site plan architect for Bo01, Professor Klas Tham, worked for Erskine for many years.

Architects Study) groups. They met to discuss the built environment, and held workshops and demonstrations to test the teachings and methods of the professions involved as well as their ideas about public participation, urban policies, and built form. The group shared tools and ideas across disciplines, making it "an opening of the disciplines" that re-interpreted the prevailing approaches to city planning. SPAS published a number of influential articles, including one that challenged the design of modernist highrise housing developments as being only for "reproduction of the work forces." The residential areas focused on the "comfort of the fathers coming home to sleep, not on the mothers and children who were using them during the day." The response to this article included rather drastic interventions in some of the housing areas in question, much to the delight of the residents and in direct opposition to the building industry and the establishment, (i.e., politicians, housing companies, and especially the architects and planners responsible). Some of the architects and planners even left the institute of architects in protest over these activist interventions, which they called "acts of vandalism to their architecture." In fact, the Architectural Press and the Institute of Architects both provided symbolic economic support to the next generation protesting against the modernist tradition.

> *Every time we build something, we manipulate the conditions of people's lives, but most planners don't know enough about this manipulation.*
> —Jan Gehl

THE EARLY COPENHAGEN STORY: THE CITY AS A LABORATORY

When starting research in 1966 on how outdoor spaces are used in cities and residential areas, it became evident to Jan that Strøget, the pedestrianized street in the city center of Copenhagen, could function as a prime study area. Between 1967 and 1968, he documented pedestrian activities and events at all times of day and in every season. As he explained, "I sat down every Tuesday and Sat-

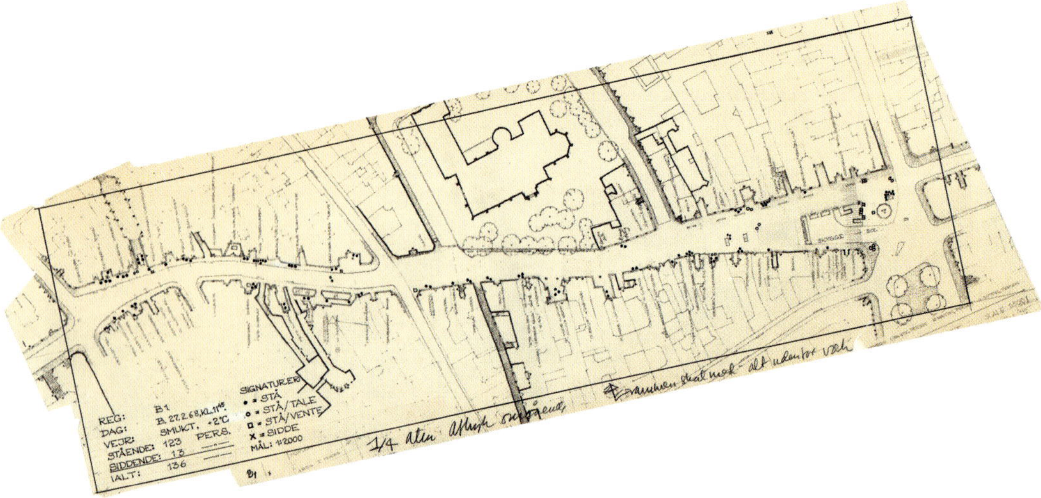

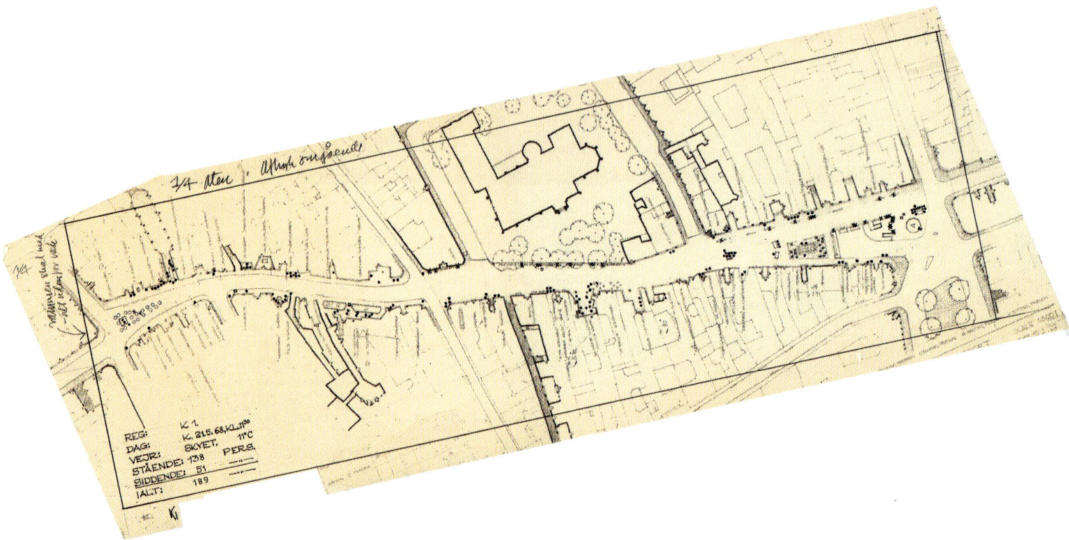

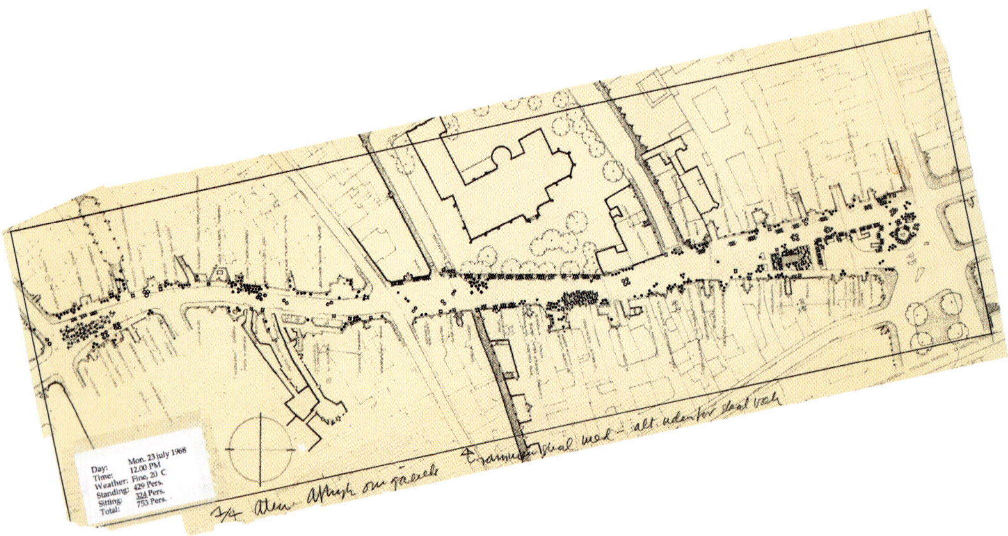

Original documents from the early studies of life on the Copenhagen's Strøget showing stationary activities around the central square in February, May, and July 1968. All recordings are made in excellent weather for the various seasons. It is clear that the number of stationary activities explodes in the summer period, making staying in the area the dominant activity, rather than walking through.

Scene from Strøget in the late 1960s. Jan is being interviewed for a radio show about his studies of the street.

Early photo (1963) from Strøget after pedestrianization. The curbs and the sidewalks are still in place, but a growing number of pedestrians are now utilizing the full width of the street.

urday, in the sun and the rain and the slush, to see what was going on in the winter and the summer, day and night, workday and weekend . . . The idea was to study the cycle of the day, the cycle of the week, and the cycle of the year to see how the rhythm of the city changed."[8]

At the time, despite a growing number of researchers becoming interested in how people use public space—namely William Holly Whyte in New York, and Christopher Alexander and Donald Appleyard in California—not many methods were known. There was a lack of other studies for Jan to refer to, so he developed his own.

Jan studued many aspects of human activity in public spaces in detail. Walking speeds, seating, and where people chose to stop and stand became a particular fascination. Jan studied how far people walked within a five-minute period, how fast various groups of pedestrians were walking, how weather influenced how people would use the street, and which seats people sat in. He found that many more people stopped in front of a construction site rather than in front of the major department stores nearby. People wanted to see other people doing things, rather than lifeless displays.

Jan published his findings in the 1968 article "Mennesker til fods" ("People on Foot").[9] The results of these extensive studies attracted considerable attention in Copenhagen, from the city planners, shop owners, and politicians. This started a dialogue on the value of life in public space that continues to this day.

The political recognition of the value of improving the quality of public space in order to encourage public life increased due to the success of Strøget, which was precisely documented by Jan's surveys. The pedestrianization of Strøget was followed, in 1968, by the next phase of pedestrianization in the city center. But not everyone was convinced by Jan's approach and studies. A 1968 newspaper article reported that he was "squandering research money" and that it was "lunacy in the research world to have someone studying public life," which must be "obvious to everyone and not worth studying." But interest in Jan's work continued to grow as he provided the hard facts and hard numbers demanded by budget processes and politicians.

PUBLISHING *LIFE BETWEEN BUILDINGS*

At the school of architecture, Jan formalized his research on public space, building on his research in Italy, his experiments with SPAS, and his detailed studies in Copenhagen. These findings formed the basis of his first book, *Life Between Buildings,* published in Danish in 1971.

Life Between Buildings was an instant success in Denmark, and was soon published in the Netherlands and Norway. In *Life Between Buildings*, Jan argues against modernist planning, maintaining that "throughout the entire history of human habitation, streets and squares had formed focal points and gathering places, but with the advent of functionalism, streets and squares were literally declared unwanted."[10] The result was the creation of monotonous and dull residential areas that do not encourage outdoor life and are unpopular with the general public. The humor and the stories of Jan's later books are not present in this first work. *Life Between Buildings* has an underlying tone of loss. It was "a matter of life and death"—a protest book about the loss of the art of making streets. (See chapter 5 for more detail on Jan's books.)

For professionals who had built such places and the academics who trained them, this was obviously challenging to hear. Also in 1971, Ingrid published her first book, *Bo-miljø* (*Living Environment*),[11] based on her research at the Danish Building Research Institute looking

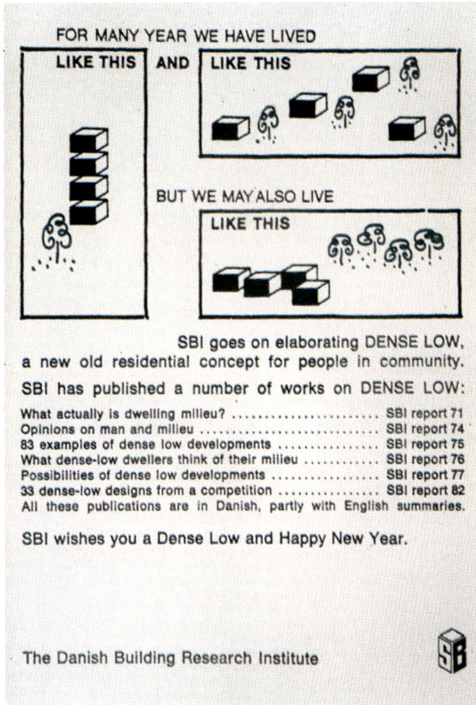

Ingrid Gehl published her very well-received book Bo miljø (Living Environment) *in 1971. The book discusses the psychological aspects of housing.*

The book was part of a major campaign organized by the Danish Building Research Institute to raise awareness about the quality of the physical environment. The intensions of this campaign are clearly reflected in the New Year card from 1971. "For many years we have lived like this (stacked) and like this (spread out), but we may also live like this (closer together). SBI wishes you a Dense, Low, and Happy New Year."

at the psychological aspects of housing. There was a similar positive reaction to Ingrid's book, which was critical of the modernist approach to architecture and planning and pointed to the need for a much more careful people-oriented response to housing needs.

While both Jan and Ingrid were immediately popular with the media, as their ideas resonated with the general public, their work was not yet seen to have much value by the majority of their colleagues.

Jan and Ingrid, in many newspaper articles, constantly emphasized why human needs and human behavior should be considered within urban planning and architecture. These articles enabled connection with a broader audience and often featured their family (now with three children) and their home, humanizing their messages and their research.

It was, however, a difficult time for Jan, both politically and professionally. Modernism still had a strong hold on planning and architecture and the School of Architecture was undergoing massive changes and restructuring due to the student revolts in the late 1960s and early 1970s.

SUMMING UP

Jan moved from his early work focused on restoring churches and designing residential developments to his initial studies of public space and the publication of his seminal work *Life Between Buildings.* From studying life in public spaces in Italy and Denmark, Jan started to develop his urban design philosophy and formalize his methodology to make people visible, which was firmly influenced by his wife Ingrid's psychological approach and by his strong belief that he could learn a great deal about design through simple, systematic observation of how people used the urban environment.

Jan Gehl
주제 : Creating a Human Quality in the City : 도시에서 인간적 삶의 창조란?
주최 : 계원조형 예술전문대학 후원 : 한국건축가협회 일시 : 1996년 10월 24일 (목) 오후4시 ~6시

3

SPREADING THE WORD

SPREADING THE WORD

"We used to say we plan at the scale of Robert Moses, but we judge ourselves by the standard of Jane Jacobs. That's not really true anymore. We judge ourselves now by Jan Gehl's standards."[12]
—Amanda Burden, Commissioner, New York City Department of Planning, 2002–2013

Jan's ideas on creating better cities for people were part of a larger, global movement toward more humanistic design during the 1960s and 1970s, inspired by the same problems and shortcomings in the ways cities were planned. Jan was influenced and exposed to some of the other players in this movement and, in turn, influenced their work. He also spent periods of time immersed in teaching and testing his ideas in Scotland, Australia, and Canada, refining his initial ideas and building confidence in the universal appicability of his ideas and in his delivery style.

INFLUENCES AND SOURCES OF INSPIRATION

Journalist and neighborhood activist Jane Jacobs (1916-2006) and Jan both believed in the need for the human dimension in planning and design. Jacobs studied the life on her street in Greenwich Village, New York, in the 1960s through observation. She argued for common sense with city planning "derived from direct observation, and related everything to peoples' daily lives."[13] Jacobs stressed the importance of the street in representing the city, recommending that one should "think of a city and what comes to mind? Its streets. If a city's streets look interesting, the city looks interesting; if they look dull, the city looks dull."[14] She explored the problems of urban design and architecture in her time, arguing that "architecture with a capital A has become more and more interested in itself, and less interested in the world that uses it."[15]

Jacobs has been extremely influential to urban planners and urban designers around the world. Her work *The Death and Life of Great American Cities* (1961) still provides vital insights into how to design vibrant cities.

In 1968, Jacobs left New York City for Toronto, where she lived for the rest of her life. When Jan was teaching at the University of Toronto in 1972 and 1973, everybody knew that the famous Jane Jacobs was living just a few blocks away. It was also well known that she did not like to be disturbed by curious academics who wandered by. Jan continued to teach his students her ideas on urbanism but refrained from disturbing her. His books were not out in English at this point and he felt that a lowly European academic should keep a respectful distance.

Therefore, although the work of Jacobs provided much inspiration to Jan, it wasn't until many years after his Toronto experience that he had any direct contact with her. The first and only personal meeting between Jane and Jan took place on her porch in Toronto in September 2001. Before this, they had exchanged

> *Architecture concerns the interaction between life and form, and only if the interaction works is it good architecture. If not, it is free-standing art, it is sculpture.*
>
> —Ken Worpole

Rightly, Jane Jacobs has been named the grandmother of humanistic city planning. Jan kept a respectful distance until rather later in his career, when contact was established through books and letters. Several framed letters can be found on the walls at the Gehl Architects office. Jan visited Jacobs in 2001, on her front porch in Toronto. They had a good conversation (mainly about the possible virtues of New Urbanism) and time for a brief photo session.

Dear Dr. Gehl

This is a much too belated thank-you for the two excellent books you sent me --Public Spaces, and Life Between Buildings. They are thoughtful, beautiful and enlightening, and I keep them on my living room table and refer to them often. My only excuse for not having written my appreciation before this is too much concentration on my part on writing my next book which will be out next spring. I'll send you a copy, as a combination apology and thanks. In the meantime, I only hope you realize how much your splendid books mean to me.

With gratitude and very best regards,

Sincerely,

Jane Jacobs

Jane Jacobs

BRIEF TIMELINE OF TWENTIETH CENTURY URBAN DESIGN: FROM MODERNIST TO HUMANISTIC DESIGN

Pre 1960s	1960s	1970s	1980s
1959 Congrès Internationaux d'Architecture Moderne (International Congress of Modern Architecture, CIAM) dissolves	**1960** Environment-behavior studies Kevin Lynch *The Image of the City* **1961** Jane Jacobs *The Death and Life of Great American Cities* **1961** Gordon Cullen *The Concise Townscape*	Start of the traffic calming movement (Joost Waal, The Netherlands) **1971** Jan Gehl (1987 English) *Life Between Buildings* **1977** Christopher Alexander et al. *A Pattern Language* **1977** Amos Rapoport *Human Aspects of Urban Form*	**1980** William H. Whyte The *Social Life of Small Urban Spaces* **1981** Donald Appleyard *Livable Streets* **1987** Christopher Alexander et al. *A New Theory of Urban Design* **1988** William H. Whyte *City: Rediscovering the Center* **1986** Clare C. Marcus and Wendy Sarkissian *Housing as if People Mattered*

A brief timeline of humanistic urban design from the pre-1960s to the 1980s. This timeline shows where and how Jan's work and theories fit within the bigger humanistic urban design happening during the same period.

a number of letters and books, and several letters from Jane Jacobs can be found framed on the walls of Jan's office in Copenhagen.

In addition to Jane Jacobs, there were others working in this field from the 1960s to the 1980s (as shown in the table above).

All of the people in the table were known to Jan, some more than others. William Holly Whyte (1917–1999) was one that Jan met on several occasions. He studied the street life and public spaces of New York. Whyte was influenced by Jan's work, particularly his methodology as documented in *Life Between Buildings,* which Whyte references in his seminal publications *The Social Life of Small Urban Spaces* (1980)[16] and *City: Rediscovering the Center* (1988).[17]

Whyte, like Jacobs, was a journalist and used various methods of observation to document the activities of people in public spaces in New York. Jan reflects that Whyte was always very curious about human life, using techniques from ethology and anthropology to study human life in cities. Particularly, he used time-lapse photography, as you would if you were observing other species. Whyte was the recipient of the first domestic National Geographic Society exhibition grant.

The two met in 1976 in New York to discuss their work, discovering that many of their findings about human behavior in public space seemed universal, whether in Italy, Copenhagen, or New York. Jan explains that this came as somewhat of a surprise to

Whyte, who firmly believed that many of his observations were firmly rooted in the culture of New Yorkers.

Whyte's work lives on with his Street Life Project, which is now the place-making organization Project for Public Spaces.

In the early 1970s, Jan met the English/ Swedish architect Ralph Erskine (1914–2005) who was a great inspiration for Jan's research. This meeting was a defining point and a source of support for Jan. Erskine, in his various residential projects, instinctively included people-friendly details, which other architects were not even thinking about in the 1970s and 1980s.

In 1971, Jan worked on an ideas competition in Stockholm with Erskine, Christopher Alexander, and several others to design a city without cars for the Märsta community near the Stockholm airport. Many interesting ideas were presented, but the main benefit of the exercise for Jan was the personal contacts that were made. Jan kept in touch with Erskine and later visited his office in Newcastle, where Erskine was working on a huge project to rehouse working-class households from rundown Victorian rowhouses to new maisonette-style housing. Erskine was undertaking this block by block. This project, known as Byker, was unique in that it did not displace families, only moving them when the new house was completed. Trees were planted from day one for the entire project so that residents would have well-grown trees, and

The Byker housing project in Newcastle upon Tyne by Ralph Erskine (1969–1981). Ralph Erskine was able to make fine architecture and yet carefully look into all the details that make a place people friendly. Characteristic of all Erskine projects was the careful treatment of the ground-floor facades, the details at eye level.

Late afternoon on a North Toronto porch, 1973.

the birds that come with them, from the moment they moved in. Jan was particularly encouraged by the reaction from the residents of Byker to Erskine. When Erskine walked through the streets, residents would come up to him and share how grateful they were that he had made their lives so much better. In his on-site project office, Erskine had a room specifically for the children and teenagers of families coming to visit. The people-sensitive design and the incremental nature of this huge urban-renewal project enabled the life of residents to be a little bit easier every day. Jan realized that this was an important goal for architecture—to make living conditions a *little bit better every day.* It also opened his eyes to the fact that you could undertake quite large-scale redevelopment in a humane way. One of Jan's favorite lessons from his meetings with Erskine is that to be a good architect, you must love people, because architecture is the framework for people's quality of life.

Strong inspiration also came from anthropologist Edward Hall's studies of human communication and how architecture affects human behavior, documented in his seminal works *The Silent Language*[18] and *The Hidden Dimension.*[19] The sociobiologist Desmond Morris also provided inspiration in Jan's early work. Some of Jan's earliest inspiration came from reading Morris' criticisms of how modern architects were completely ignoring human behavior.[20]

GOING GLOBAL (1971–1978): SCOTLAND, CANADA, AND AUSTRALIA

The release of *Life Between Buildings* in Denmark in 1971 coincided with a period of uncertainty at the School of Architecture. At this time, Jan was unable to teach due to political interference. It was the "dawn of the student revolt and the school of architecture was an extremely difficult place to undertake research if it was not strongly related to political economy." In this context, studying life between buildings was considered to be "an

utter waste of time, and making better cities could even be seen as a potential delay on the road to revolution!" With these challenges at the school of architecture, and a desire to work globally, Jan embarked on a period of international research and teaching, accepting many invitations to be a visiting professor. Recognition of his work was growing internationally, with the help of his many lectures and his Danish book, which luckily had an English-language extended abstract.

This was the start of his international focus and the growth of his international networks and connections. Between 1971 and 1978, Jan spent several periods teaching and continuing his research as a visiting professor in Scotland, Australia, and Canada.

Jan's research continued to focus on how built form influences life in public spaces. In this period, his research was mainly focused on public space in residential areas, particularly the influence of the transition zones in the form of front porches (verandas), front yards, and fences between people's homes and the street. He conducted research experiments, testing methods with groups of students at the universities where he lectured. The time away from his normal teaching duties gave him an opportunity to immerse himself in his research.

In 1971, Jan was invited to Edinburgh, Scotland, where he lectured about life between buildings at the School of Architecture at Heriot Watt University. Much later, in the 1980s, architect David Sim, now partner and creative director at Gehl Architects, studied architecture at the same school. Sim said that the influence of Jan at the university was still very apparent—Jan brought cities alive for people. For many years, video recordings of Jan's lectures were shown to the students, so his ideas were ever present. In 1992, Jan was awarded an honorary doctorate degree by the university.

After Edinburgh, Ingrid and Jan were very interested in going to New Zealand to take

Living in North Toronto in 1972–73 was a great experience for the Gehl family. The porches in front of every house played a major role in creating the very friendly atmosphere in the neighborhood.

up an appointment at the University of Auckland. But the journey proved too expensive for a family with three children. So the family instead went to Toronto, Canada, where Jan was a guest professor at the University of Toronto (1972–1973). In addition to being the coordinator for the fifth-year students, Jan and Ingrid presented a series of guest lectures about the "social dimension in architecture and urban planning"[21] which was extremely well received. There was a huge demand from the students, and very soon, the sessions had standing room only. It appeared that people came from very far away to Toronto to hear the lectures. This overwhelming interest revealed to Ingrid and Jan that they were "on to something"—that their approach to urban design and planning based on observation and the cooperation and mutual learning between the disciplines was appealing to other researchers. It appeared that humanistic urban design had universal appeal, and it was also quite apparent that the research and applications in Denmark, particularly in housing research, were at that point far ahead of the local North American scene.

The success of the Toronto lectures led to lecture invitations from all the other Canadian architecture schools and the first invitations from the US. Indeed the interest was very

Street studies in Melbourne. Jan with the study group from the University of Melbourne, April 1976.

Above: Street ballet as seen in a terrace house area in South Melbourne, 1976. As the social life unfolds, the father, who is repairing the roof, is in danger of falling due to his keen interest in following the events!

Street studies in Melbourne 1976

The focus for the studies was the interface between public and private spaces in residential areas. It was proven beyond any doubt that the "soft interfaces" played a major role in the life of the streets. Sixty-nine percent of all activities occurred on or near the front yards. Only 31% occurred in the street spaces.

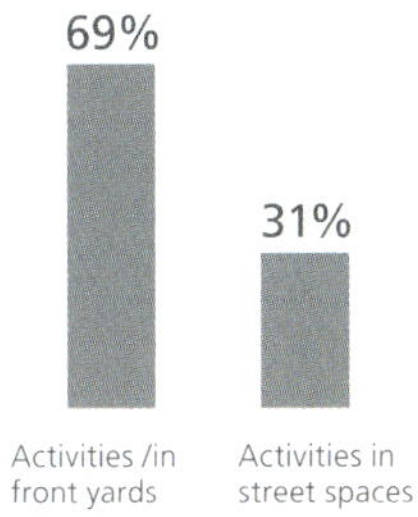

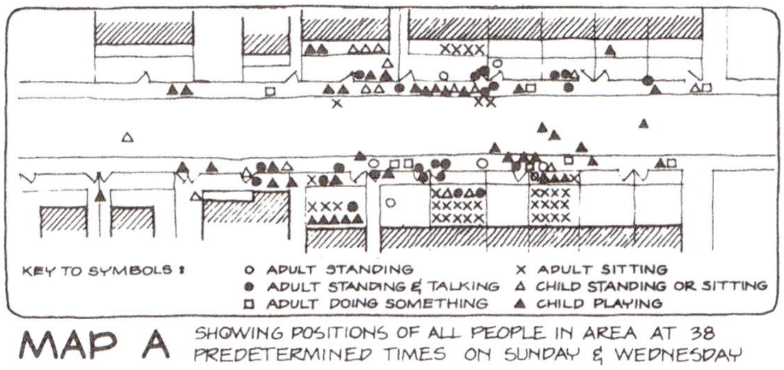

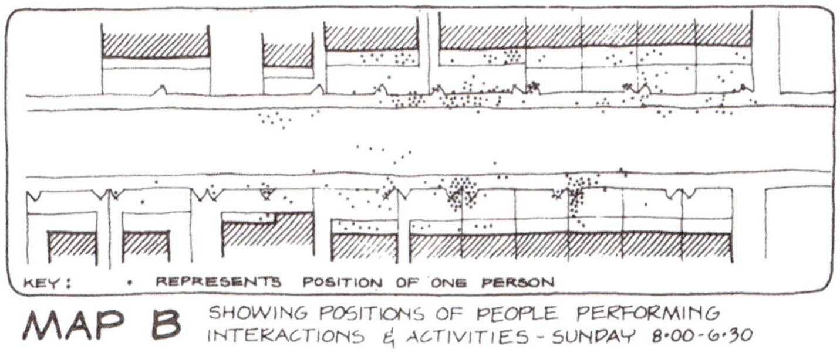

Student (discretely) studying street life. The students would mumble something on the importance of studying traffic safety in residential streets and the residents would express their full support.

widespread, and the spring of 1973 turned out to be a very busy period for both Ingrid and Jan. Visits to the University of Michigan and the University of Kansas in early 1973 were Jan's first introductions to the American scene. He recalls that he was very surprised to realize that everyone talked about safety in cities. Sidewalk safety was not an issue in Toronto or in Scandinavia at this time.

One of the important topics Jan studied while in Canada was the role of the front porch. He tells the story of walking home in the North Toronto inner suburb where he and the family were living, where all the homes had front porches. After a long day of teaching, he would be invited in by one after the other of his neighbors to enjoy their front porches, resulting in one too many martinis and a wobbly walk home! Jan uses this story in his presentations as an illustration of the

Street studies in Kitchener/Waterloo, Ontario, 1977

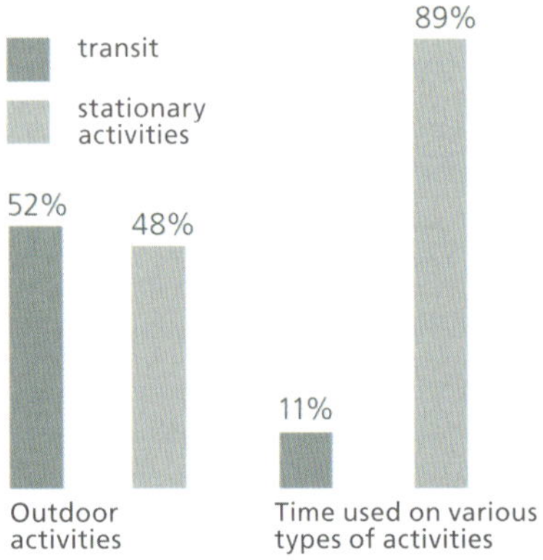

In 1977, another street life study was conducted, this time organized with students from University of Waterloo, Canada. In total, twelve streets in the cities of Waterloo and Kitchener were surveyed. The main emphasis in this survey was to study the time used for different activities and how that influenced the liveliness of the streets. Going to and from the houses constituted 52% of all activities, but these transit activities were all of short duration and actually meant little for the activity levels in the streets.

Studying street life in West Australia turned out to be quite a dull experience. The photo illustrates two of the highlights: A neighbor waters his front lawn with a sprinkler and the school children walk home from school, on the traffic street (where they definitely were not supposed to be).

Suburban studies in Perth, 1978

Visiting the University of West Australia in 1978, Jan conducted a study of a new traffic safety area, praised because pedestrian activities and traffic were completely separated. As suspected, it proved not to be as efficient as the traffic engineers had predicted. Also in this case people chose the shortest routes and children preferred to play where most activities occurred, namely on the traffic routes. What should have provided more safety actually turned out to be less safe. Below: One of the many activity mappings at Crestwood.

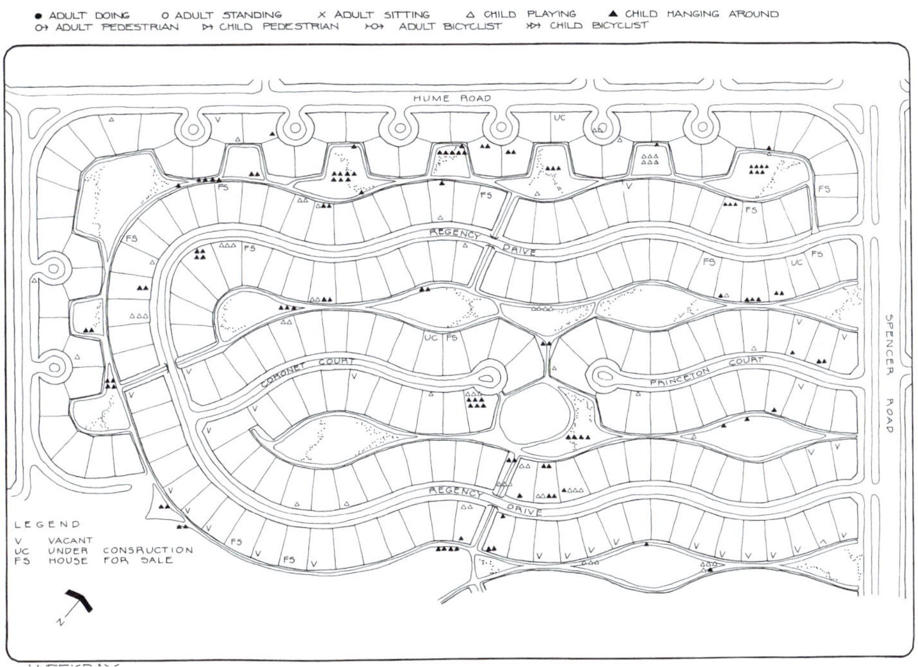

importance of the public-private interface to sense of community and neighborliness.

In 1976, there began a very long period of engagement with, and influence on, Australian cities. At this point, Jan was invited as a Nell Norris Research Fellow to the School of Architecture at the University of Melbourne where he taught a number of courses focused on the interface between the design of residential streets and the types and extent of activities carried out in them. That Australian autumn, Jan and 33 students studied the difference in activities between older and newer residential streets using behavioral maps and diaries. This study was published in the booklet "The Interface Between Public and Private Territories in Residential Areas."[22] The 17 streets selected were diverse in terms of design but also in ethnicity, income level, and other characteristics. This study highlighted

Street studies in Melbourne, Sydney, and Adelaide, 1978

During a visit to the University of Melbourne and RMIT in 1978, a study of three types of streets was conducted: pedestrian streets, pedestrian streets with some traffic, and ordinary traffic streets with sidewalks. Not surprisingly, great differences in people's activities and behavior were found when comparing the life in pedestrian streets and in the traffic streets. It was very interesting to note that just a little bit of traffic or the occasional tram going through a pedestrian street had a very strong negative impact on the street life.

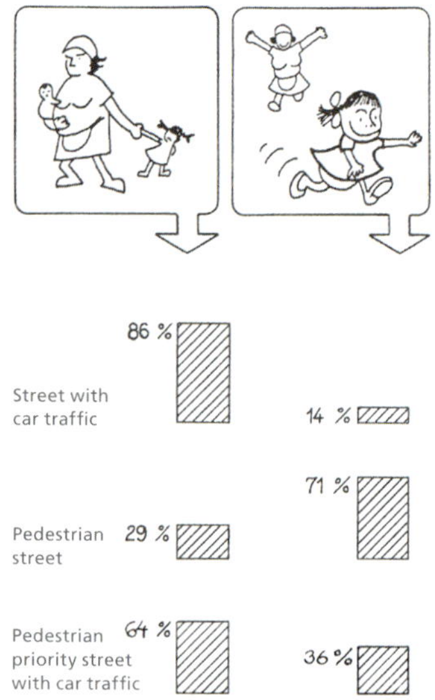

The price of fear: Distribution of children 0–6-years-old in Australian traffic and pedestrian streets. Almost no children are allowed to run freely on the sidewalks on traffic streets, while almost no children are held by the hand on pedestrian streets.

The street benches in Melbourne were extremely crowded (left). The city architect was persuaded to loan another 100 park benches to the study group. The benches were duly placed according to a plan made by the students, and just a day later a doubling of the people sitting in Melbourne was recorded.

the importance of the interface between the private realm (the residential home, especially the front yard and building facades) and the public realm (the street). The older streets generally featured a small front yard bordered by a low fence where it met the sidewalk. The new streets were characterized by setbacks with extensive lawns surrounding the house. The study found that both types of streets had many weekend activities, but the activities undertaken were distinctly different. In the older streets, the activities tended to be social and recreational activities, such as eating, drinking tea, or just hanging around enjoying the outdoors. In the newer suburbs, the activities tended to be working in the garden. In the newer areas, the setbacks did not facilitate interactions with the neighbors or the infrequent passers-by walking along the sidewalk.[23] They found that areas with a soft interface, that is a gradual transition as provided by low fences, small front yards, and small front verandas, were able to facilitate a higher level of interaction between people. Jan and the students determined that "this stepwise buffer zone" enabled "transition from public to private, with various built-in possibilities for protecting privacy as well as for engaging in social activities in a relaxed and easily controlled way." In this soft transition, "an array of in-between possibilities is left open."[24] Co-authors Thornton and Brack, reflecting on this study, mentioned the use of the words "neighborliness," "happiness," and "friendship" by Jan in reference to "characteristics that might be affected by the built form,"[25] all in stark contrast to most architectural or planning language of the time. The theme of soft edges has been recurring throughout Jan's research and has been applied to commercial as well as residential streets.

In 1977, Jan returned to Canada to teach at the School of Architecture at the University of Waterloo, south of Toronto. Here he undertook similar studies as in Melbourne, looking at the activity patterns in 12 residential streets with a mix of detached and semi-detached houses. This study was important as it highlighted that it is not only the number of activities undertaken in the public space, but also the duration of the activities that is important. The study found that the most common activity was the many journeys to and from the home. However, this activity was generally undertaken quickly and only accounted for approximately ten percent of the "life in the streets" as observed in the street.[26] Activities such as sitting, watching, children playing, and gardening, all of longer duration, were found to be much more important to the liveliness of the street, accounting for 90 percent of the activity levels on those streets.

While this may seem obvious in retrospect, at the time it was a new insight about the use of public space. This understanding of duration of activities as "a decisive factor for life in public space" continues to be explored by Jan.[27]

In late 1978, Jan returned to Melbourne to teach at the University of Melbourne and at the School of Architecture at the Royal Melbourne Institute of Technology. Here, again with teams of students, he compared types of streets, this time looking at pedestrian streets, mixed-pedestrian and tram streets, and ordinary traffic streets using pedestrian counting, behavioral mapping, and observation. Streets in Melbourne, Sydney, and Adelaide were studied, and spectacular differences in behavior were found. The studies found that the presence of even a few trams or cars within the street led to immediate changes in people's activity patterns sparked by a steep rise in concern for personal safety or the safety of the children present.

Based on the 1976 studies in Melbourne, Jan was also invited in 1978 to teach at the University of Western Australia (UWA) in Perth. At UWA, Jan and his architectural students studied the newly completed suburban residential area of Crestwood Estate in Thornlie. This estate featured contemporary, state-of-the-art traffic safety design built following Radburn design principles, which are based on the idea of total separation of vehicular and pedestrian traffic. In this newly designed area, footpaths were separated from the roads carrying automotive traffic throughout the estate, with vehicle access on the street side and pedestrian access on the park side. This was seen as an innovative way to improve quality of life and safety. The estate featured significantly more public open space than traditional Perth subdivisions of the time, with each house facing both a street and a park (traditional designs at the time had the houses facing the streets only).

Through observational studies of the estate, Jan and his students found that the majority of activities were not where the traffic engineers expected them to be—people invariably took the shortest routes, and children preferred to be where most things were happening—which was on the vehicle access streets. As a result of this study, the remaining land in the suburb was later developed along more conventional suburban design ideas and the streets within the area were reclaimed as the main orientation for the housing. Several other suburbs in Western Australia with this modernist concept of separation have also abandoned their inside-out design and returned to traditional streets, and the design idea has not been used again.

DEVELOPING A UNIVERSAL MESSAGE

During this period, Jan developed his unique presentation style, telling stories using real people and real-life examples. Stories and photos of people using public space, often in interesting and amusing ways, is now characteristic of his communication. Particularly important is his use of photos of people, enabling viewers to picture themselves in those spaces. This is very different from traditional architectural presentations, which most often show buildings or concept drawings with anonymous people, if people are included at all. Jan's lectures were "a spicy mix of opinion and fact, for which Jan makes no apologies."[28]

SUMMING UP

Jan Gehl is a giant in the contemporary history of urban design. But like all giants of history, he rises on the shoulders of others. However, Jan is unique in that he not only is a powerful contributor to the ideas that challenged modernist design thinking, he also is a provider of the solutions. He showed us how to do something about a problem in a series of practical steps. But before he could do this, he needed to develop the confidence that his observations about people in cities were universal. Jan discovered that "cultures and climates differ all over the world, but people are the same. They'll gather in public if you give them a good place to do it."

Example 1: Using photos to tell a story

A recurring feature of Jan's lectures is the use of very telling photos or short, humorous stories drawing on experiences from his life. The following examples are all stories from Jan's lectures.

What do you do when the architect forgot to give you access to the garden? You just bring your own ladder and carry down whatever you need for an outing!

Sign found in Cologne, Germany. Text probably means: Mothers carefully hold onto your daughters in this area!

Sign found in Poland. Sign probably advises pedestrians to keep their arms straight down while walking on this sidewalk!

Rule of thumb: If there is more life behind a bench than in front of it, the bench will either not be used or used in new, interesting ways!

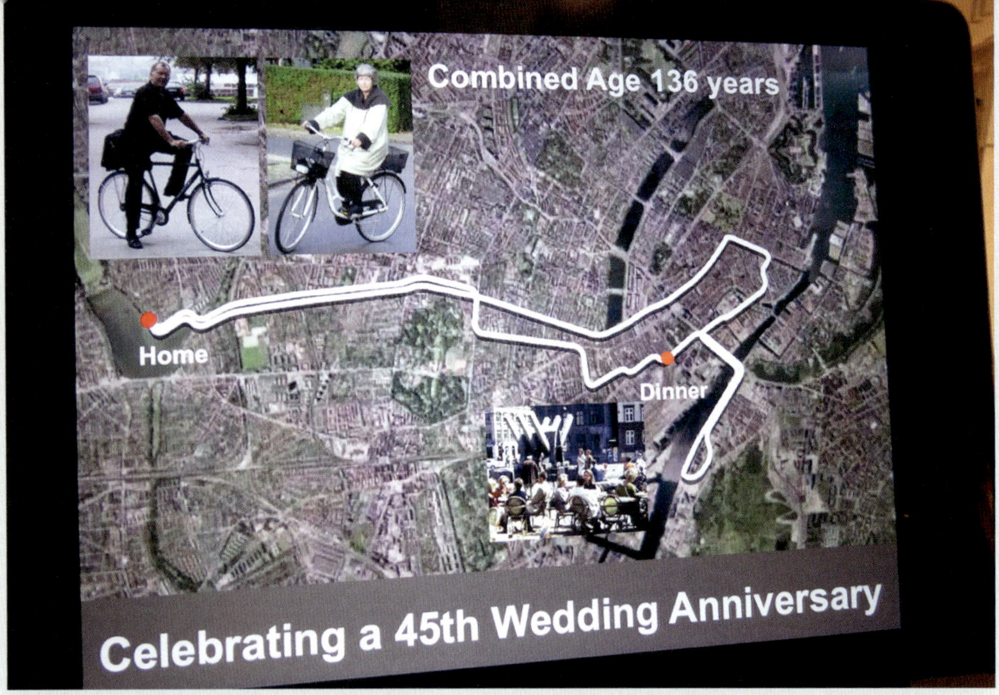

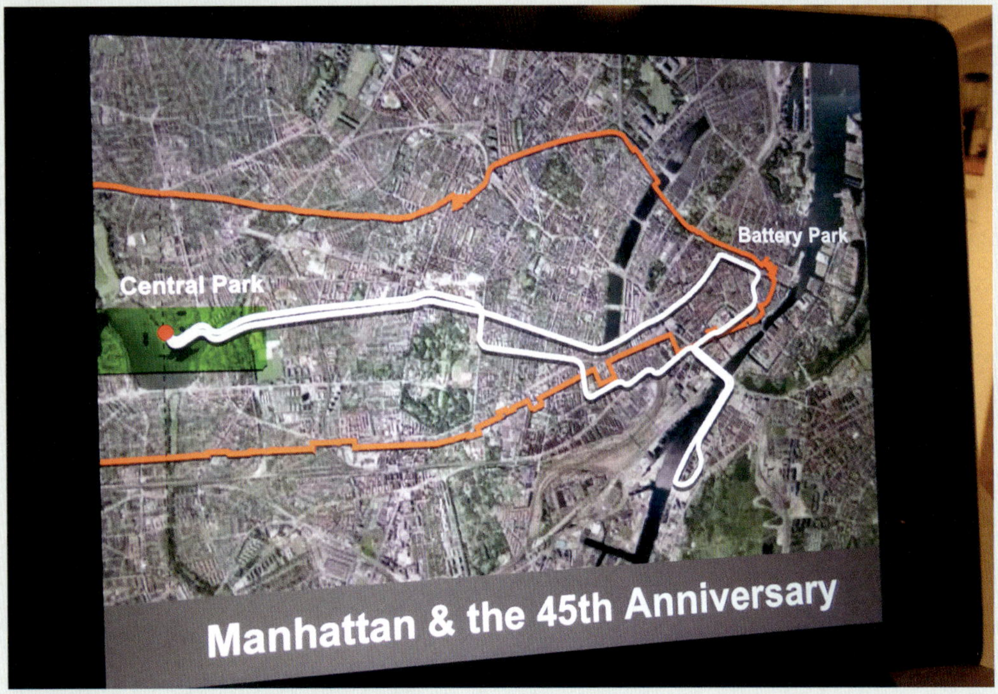

Example 2: The 45th Anniversary

Jan's story about his forty-fifth wedding anniversary demonstrates a truly bike-friendly city. For this occasion, Jan and Ingrid, both near 70-years-old (one less than, one more than), bicycled from their home to dinner in New York City. With a few detours and stops, they rode past interesting areas in the downtown area. By the end of this outing, they had covered 20 kilometers, but it felt like nothing because it was so easily made on dedicated bicycle lanes. This trip illustrates the ease of cycling in the city, enabling uncomplicated transport as well as uncomplicated ways to be part of city life. Jan uses a map of their route, overlaid on cities he is visiting, to demonstrate both the lack of cycling infrastructure in other cities and the possibilities for those cities.

Example 3. Spontaneous vs. Planned Activities

Street scene from Melbourne. Having one square meter of space next to the door is invariably more useful than ten square meters around the corner.

A story of two trombones. One trombone is nicely packed in its case. To play, you have to open, assemble, and tune the instrument. You may even have to find the music and put it up on its stand before you can get going—a complicated operation needing careful planning. The other trombone is just lying around, assembled, and tuned. Everything is ready to go. Jan always felt guilty because he did not have time to practice on his instrument. But if the trombone was ready and did not have to be unpacked and prepared, then Jan found that he would actually play much more. He could play spontaneously, whenever the inspiration (or need for a break) overcame him. Jan uses this example to explain the importance of making room for spontaneous activities—things you can just do, rather than having to plan them in advance. This is important to understanding the differences between living in an apartment in a highrise building (where every outdoor visit has to be planned) and living at ground level, with a good porch facing the street.

Vanjazztic

Jan always wanted to play the trombone. In 1979, he finally came around to buying one. In no time, the other boys (and one girl) in the neighborhood also got hold of instruments. Their new band, Vanjazztic, was born. The band was named after Vanløse, their neighborhood. It was a group of seven musicians playing traditional New Orleans-inspired jazz. All were in their early forties and had seen their own children become teenagers. A coach was hired and, with his help and with some more experience, the group began to play real music. Playing with Vanjazztic for some 37 years now, has been one of Jan's most cherished activities. The group has participated in street parades, gospel concerts, the Walk 21 Conference street walk, birthdays, anniversaries, parties, and so on.

Example 4: Do you have a baby boom in Copenhagen?

In October 2009, Jan was invited to Vietnam in connection with the publication of Life Between Buildings *in Vietnamese. On this occasion, Jan met Mrs. Lan, an employee of the Danish embassy in Hanoi. She had just visited Copenhagen and was convinced that there was a real baby boom in Denmark. Jan could not understand this. There was absolutely no baby boom. In fact, there was a slight decline in the birthrate. After a while, it became clear that Mrs. Lan had just noticed a large number of children in the city. There was no baby boom, just a city with many children in the streets, squares, and parks. Children were walking on sidewalks, playing in parks and squares, and many were on bicycles or being transported by bikes all over the city. It is a good city for children.*

Whenever you see a city with many children and elderly people in the streets and squares, it is a sure sign of city quality.

HOW TO STUDY PUBLIC LIFE
GEHL & SVARRE
HOW TO STUDY PUBLIC LIFE

4

COPENHAGEN AS LABORATORY

COPENHAGEN AS LABORATORY

"Without the public life studies from the School of Architecture, we politicians wouldn't have had the courage to implement the many projects to increase the attractiveness of the city"
—Bente Frost, Mayor for Building and Planning Copenhagen (1994–1997)

After the various visits to other continents and universities, Jan resumed his teaching and research work at the School of Architecture at the Royal Danish Academy of Fine Arts in Copenhagen in 1976. He again focused on the changes happening within the city.

In 1978, architect Lars Gemzøe, who became a long-time colleague of Jan's, joined Jan's research and teaching team. Together they formed the core of the research group studying Copenhagen. After a period of increasing collaboration with the City of Copenhagen, a "good town-and-gown partnership began in earnest."

This is a period in which all of the elements of Jan's research began to come together. Lars and Jan, and others in the urban design department, endeavored to visit every city

In the 1950s, all of the 18 squares in central Copenhagen were parking lots. In the years following the closing of Strøget, the main street, all 18 have been turned into people squares. Below: Gammeltorv/Nytorv in 1956 and in 2006.

Until 1980, Nyhavn, the prominent waterfront street, was a parking place for some 90 cars. In 1980, this street was made car-free and was immediately taken over by pedestrian activity. Ever since, it has been the most popular public space in the city.
Top: Nyhavn as a parking place in 1979.
Below: Nyhavn as an attractive and very popular pedestrian space in 2007.

in Denmark, evaluating their public spaces. This later resulted in the book *Bedre byrum* (*Better Urban Spaces*), published in 1990, which came to have a substantial influence on public-space policies in the Danish provincial cities.

THE 1986 PUBLIC SPACE PUBLIC LIFE SURVEY

As mentioned, Copenhagen, like most other cities at the time, had been overtaken by modernist planning, which focused on automobiles, not on people. In 1956, the city opened its first freeway, which travelled through the northern Copenhagen suburbs. The medieval city center was soon filled with cars, pushing people out of the public spaces. Plans for building more freeways across the historic city were prepared and the city faced an auto-centric future. Although the city also began to experiment

University visits

The 1980s were mainly a period of working in Scandinavia, although Jan continued his international academic collaborations, including guest-teaching Donald Appleyard's course at the University of California, Berkeley in 1983, in the term just after Appleyard was hit and killed by a car in Greece. This was an important period because Berkeley housed another of the very few centers for humanistic urban design research in the world. In Berkeley, Jan met and worked with kindred souls such as Allan Jacobs, Clare Cooper Marcus, and Peter Bosselmann. Strong friendships were formed, and Peter Bosselmann was to have an important role in Jan's future work as "a soulmate and critic" for the books Jan published beginning in 1996. (In all of Jan's books, you can find Bosselmann referenced and often listed with the research team.)

Another visit to Berkeley was arranged in 1985, followed by visits to several other universities globally. The 1986 visit to Dresden in East Germany, in particular, stands out. These two weeks of teaching, in one of the final years before the Berlin Wall came down, were especially interesting because of what Jan describes as the general apathy and lack of belief in the future felt by the students coupled with the overwhelming interest that they showed in learning about the human dimension in architecture and planning—a perspective that was completely neglected in socialist East Germany. Jan remembers that the professors were not amused, but certainly the students were. The visit came about as part of an academic exchange program, which enabled East German professors to visit, and to shop, in the West, an idea that was very popular among the East German professors. Teaching in Dresden was not popular, however, with the Danish academics, but Jan volunteered to go because he had heard how eager the students were to learn about the human approach to architecture.

Further teaching and research visits to Guadalajara, Mexico (1983); Wroclaw, Poland in the "Solidarity" period (1987); Jakarta, Indonesia (2004); Cape Town, South Africa, reborn after Apartheid (2001); and San José, Costa Rica (2006) were interwoven with the academic work in Copenhagen in order to broaden Jan's experience and knowledge of what was going on in various parts of the world.

"Bicycling in Berkeley" was the theme for the course Jan taught at the University of California, Berkeley in 1983.

Visiting Indonesia in 2000.

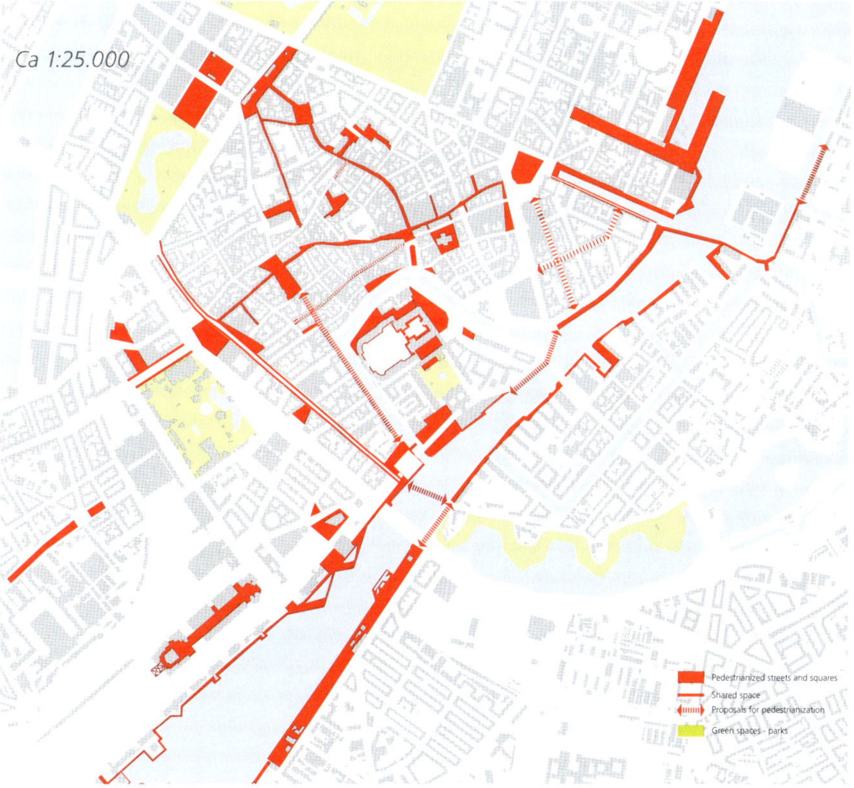

Developing the people spaces in central Copenhagen from 1962 until 2016, and a little bit beyond.
Above: The people spaces available after the transformation of Strøget in 1962.
Below: The people landscape by 2016 (including projects in progress). Year after year, Copenhagen has been made more and more people-friendly.

The development of people spaces in Copenhagen has happened in three distinct phases: Phase one (1960–1980) focused on pedestrian streets and pedestrian-priority streets. Emphasis was put on walking and promenading.

Phase two (1980–2000) focused on creating good places to stay in the city. Emphasis was put on sitting to enjoy the city, café culture, and cultural events.

Phase three (2000 and onward) has been a period with increasing focus on sports, activities, and play. Emphasis has been on movement and activities of all sorts.

with pedestrian and cycling infrastructure in the city core in the 1960s, and even had some big successes as Jan had found in his study of the pedestrianization of Strøget, modernist planning continued to prevail in the city, including the removal of the last remaining tram lines in 1972.

A turning point in the momentum came from the oil crisis in 1973. Denmark was severely impacted by the oil embargo. The country was forced to react by introducing "car-free Sundays." The shortage gave momentum to the civil movements trying to stop the development of freeways through Copenhagen. A string of modernist plans included building freeways, including City Plan West approved in 1958, and Søringen (The Lake Ring), approved in 1964. If implemented, the result would have been a 12-lane freeway with an interchange at the lakes near the residential neighborhood of Vesterbro. This plan required filling in part of the much-loved city lakes and removing parts of an existing residential area. Civil protest against the plan and against modernist tower blocks intensified. Jan's close friend, Michael Varming, ran a clever campaign using floats in the lake to demonstrate how much of the lakes would actually be swallowed up by the proposed freeways. Other protests to the proposed changes demonstrated the impact of new highrise hotels using large hot air balloons. The freeway and the modernist city transformations were cancelled by the Copenhagen city government in 1974.[29] The Danish national government reacted to this change of plan by withdrawing transport funding, hence the city could only undertake low-cost projects such as bicycle lanes. From this point, the City concentrated on improving public space, protecting the environment, and encouraging cycling over car use.[30]

As covered in chapter 2, Jan spent most of the 1967–1968 season observing, day-after-day, how the new car-free areas in the city were working for people. The initial studies, published in *Arkitekten* in 1968, documented the success of the early pedestrianization schemes. In 1973, substantial extensions were introduced, creating a pedestrianized

In recent years, the City of Copenhagen has steadily been publishing planning documents that incorporate public life as a major element in their city planning. "A Metropolis for People," the strategy document approved by the city council in 2009, states that Copenhagen will be aiming to be the best city in the world for people.

network from one end of the city center to the other. Around this time, many other cities around the world also pedestrianized their main streets. The difference was that these were usually only a few streets for one or two blocks. In Copenhagen, the car-free streets formed a network running through the city center, creating a solid invitation for walking.

During the 1970s and 1980s, the city shifted emphasis from pedestrian streets to creating more car-free squares and plazas, including removing cars from Nyhavn, an attractive waterfront street, and turning it into a linear square. This waterfront street has increasingly become iconic for the city and a beacon for visitors.

Jan and the research team from the School of Architecture continued documenting how the city was used by people, and how the various additions to the car-free network were received. These smaller studies culminated in a large study, published in 1986 in *Arkitekten*. These studies would collectively become Jan's signature methodology—the Public Space Public Life survey. With these studies, Copenhagen became the first city in the world to document the people's use of the city in a systematic way.

The 1986 study found that the number of people walking on the main streets was essentially the same as in the 1960s—the streets filled to capacity shorty after being pedestrianized. What had changed, remarkably, was the number of people staying and spending time in the streets and squares. The data showed a much more lively city center. Jan systematically documented how Copenhagen, in a step-by-step process, had transformed the central city area into a definitively more people-friendly zone.

The 1986 study became the "catalyst for closer cooperation between researchers at the school of architecture and the politicians and planners at city hall."[31] Whenever

One of the most important new public spaces from the current phase emphasizing activity, sports, and play is the Islands Brygge Harbour Park, which incorporates a swimming facility placed directly in the harbor. Over the years, the water in the harbor has become so clean that swimming has become possible.

Mennesker til fods (People on Foot), 1968

Byliv 1986 (Public Life 1986)

Byens rum – byens liv, København 1996 (Public Spaces Public Life—Copenhagen, 1996)

Det nye byliv (New City Life) 2006

Four major studies of the public life in Copenhagen have been conducted between 1968 and 2006 by research teams from the School of Architecture and have in a gradual process obtained a major influence on the public space policies of the city.

the city government implemented a change to the public space, Jan, with students and research fellows, documented the changes to public life. Many workshops and meetings were held throughout the many years around the presentation of the public life studies, enabling widespread discussion of the changes that were happening within the city. The city government was encouraged in its people-oriented planning direction by the research findings from the school of architecture. Through this process, the school of architecture provided the ideology and documentation and the city government gained the inspiration and courage to "lay the stones." This collaboration enabled continuous testing and refinement of the City of Copenhagen's public space program. Jan explains the relationship in a booklet he wrote while at the Center for Public Space Research: "public space and public life studies provided the ideologies and collected the data concerning how people-oriented spaces worked, and how the life of the city developed accordingly, while the planners and politicians of City of Copenhagen have been able to use the ideologies and research findings in their arguments and planning."[32]

The politicians and the city planners enjoyed Jan's work because it gave evidence that the citizens of Copenhagen were happy with the policies and projects that provided attractive public spaces in the city. And this political success led to more and more commitments favoring pedestrians and public life within the city, which continue to this day.

The Copenhagen study became a model for later studies around the world, though it was orginally only intended for local audiences. It was driven by genuine curiosity about how people used city spaces. In this process, Jan developed a formula that, as the future developments would show, could be taken to cities around the world: study the city, create a

The Center for Public Space Research

In 2003, a generous grant from the Realdania Foundation for the built environment enabled the Center for Public Space Research at the School of Architecture to be much expanded. Realdania saw a need for supporting and developing the people-oriented planning research conducted by the center. Here, keeping with his international focus, Jan taught urban design courses in English and attracted a wide array of international research students.

It was a very active period. The center was staffed by some 10 researchers including two PhD students, and conducted a number of studies such as "Close Encounters with Buildings"[41] and "Pass or Stay, 2006." An important research project carried out at the center was to conduct yet another Public Space Public Life survey of Copenhagen, continuing the remarkable tradition of documenting public life every tenth year over a period of, by now, four decades. The findings from this survey were published in the book *New City Life* (2006; Gehl with Gemzøe, Kirknæs, and Søndergaard) (see chapter 5).[42]

In between these activities, the center hosted two mayor international conferences—WALK 21-Cities for People in 2004 and Public Spaces Public Life in 2006—along with a number of courses, seminars, and workshops all focused on public space and public life.

In 2006, after three years as center director, Jan turned 70 and retired gracefully from the School of Architecture, in accordance with the retirement rules for state employees. At this point, the new directors from within the School of Architecture who took over the center wanted to change the focus from people-oriented research to form-oriented research, specifically related to landscape architecture and design. Realdania, for this reason, withdrew its funding, which was specifically given for "people studies." In this turmoil, most of the former students and researchers quit working at the center and moved to Gehl Architects, which was by now well established. This gave the firm the capacity to grow substantially and also to combine consultancy work with research work.

Just after his retirement in 2006, a farewell party was organized at which the center's crew posed for a group photo. Jan frequently referred to the group as "the dream team," carefully assembled over several years.
Front row, from left: Ai Sakurai, Helle Juul, Sofie Andersen, Jan Gehl, Camilla Ricter Friis van Deurs, Britt S. Søndergaard, and Sia Kirknæs. Back row, from left: Solveig Reigstad, Director Rob Adams, Susanne Andersen (visiting scholar from the City of Melbourne), Javier Corvalán, Lars Gemzøe, a guest student, and Mikkel Mindegaard-Müllertz.

The edge—where building and city meet

Stopping to chat

Entering and leaving

Walking alongside

Standing alongside

Taking a break by

Standing in doorways

Shopping next to

Interacting with

Looking at displays

Sitting on

Sitting next to

Looking in and out of

"Close Encounters with Buildings," a major study conducted by the center, was published in 2004. This study surveyed a number of interactions between public life and ground-floor frontages. Shown on this page is an overview of 12 different encounters between people and buildings.

WORKING WITH JAN GEHL

by Camilla Richter-Friis van Deurs, PhD
Partner, Gehl Architects

The first time I ever heard someone in the School of Architecture speaking about people was at a course led by Jan Gehl on how to prepare your projects and presentations. Naturally, this course was in no way directly associated with the field of urban design, but it was typical for how Jan thought about teaching—that it was as imperative to be able to communicate the project as to develop the content of the project. Jan used the course as an opportunity to introduce his theories about how people interacted with the built environment—and even the dynamics of how we interacted together in the classroom explaining Sven-Ingvar Andersson´s 4th law: *"Always book an auditorium that is smaller than the amount of spectators you expect. That way, they will all feel so lucky to even get in to the room and be standing up against the walls reminding themselves to come early next time. This will lead them to believe that you are an excellent lecturer."* Jan compared this to designing good public spaces where the size of the spaces should always be a little too small if they are to feel intimate and to adhere to a human scale. Jan´s lectures were magical and memorable. Armed with a double deck of slides and a myriad of anecdotes, he would speak about basic human social needs, arrogant (male) modernist architects, and personal observations of life unfolding in the streets.

The following year, I started my graduate degree at the Department of Urban Design (Bybygning) to peruse this undefined "urban design thing," which, in the eyes of my fellow classmates and former teachers in the architecture building department, was just about the worst career move I could make. We were a collection of lost souls in Bybygning, all of us interested in something other than the buildings themselves—the entirety of the urban realm, larger social or societal problems, or planning issues—at a time when neo-modernism, Japanese architecture and high-tech constructions were all the rage of the establishment. Jan was the figure of cohesion in the department, and often also the shoulder to weep on in times of personal troubles, although he was not always there, travelling quite a bit around the world to attend conferences and teach in one of the many universities where he was a guest professor. However, for us as students at Bybygning, Jan´s international connections were one of the benefits. We were the department in the School of Architecture with the highest amount of foreign guest students and an international, dynamic teaching environment at a time when most of the other professors would not even dream of conducting a lecture in English. Jan had a special place in his heart for students from Greenland, the Faeroe Islands, and Iceland and was deeply engaged in the urban developments there emphasizing the need for regional architecture and planning in accordance with local culture, history, landscape, and climate. When it came to organizing internships, Jan would always say, "Just point to anywhere on the map where you would like to have an internship and I will make it happen," and most of the time, this was actually possible. Many of Jan's students today work or live abroad thanks to Jan's generosity in sharing his extensive international and academic network, and in ensuring that these connections were passed on to the next generations of scholars and young professionals.

Jan always engaged the students in his research, books, and movies. We stood on street corners and counted pedestrians, and we drew endless numbers of maps of cities and public spaces for illustrations in the books *Public Space Public Life* and *New City Spaces*. The research was in that way very alive, and not purely an academic project behind closed office doors. Jan seemed to us to be a professor who genuinely cared about us and the urban design profession, but also gave the impression of a grand personality with humor and wit.

After graduating from Bybygning, I continued to work as a landscape architect until 2003 when Jan, after receiving a grant from The Realdania Foundation, had the opportunity to establish the Center for Public Space Research. Jan was always very loyal to his former students: Solvejg Reigstad, Lotte Kaefer, Sia Kirknæs and I joined the Center at the School of Architecture to support the research development together with Jan's longtime friend and co-worker Lars Gemzøe. Jan was instrumental in establishing two PhD positions at the center where Birgitte Bundesen Svarre, who later became co-author of *How to Study Public Life*, and myself, studied public life in suburban environments and newer housing developments, thereby continuing the studies Jan had started in *Life Between Buildings*.

The spirit of the center was exciting: international conferences, books, foreign guest researchers. But unfortunately, there was very little interaction with the rest of the staff or students in the Copenhagen School of Architecture. After five years, the center closed and all the researchers there, including myself, shifted into the private practice, in my case Gehl Architects, leaving no traces of Jan's 40 years of academic work and the field of urban design in the Copenhagen School of Architecture, something I believe Jan always felt as quite a disappointment.

New York, Singapore, Sydney, Melbourne, London, Lublin, and Kaliningrad. These are some of the projects I have had the pleasure of working on with Jan during my time at Gehl Architects. Jan is always concerned about the projects he is involved with, from the overarching political strategies right down to correcting spelling errors or defining the graphics communication of the reports and in this way; he has brought his unique storytelling skills into the projects at the practice, making the projects relevant and engaging while always keeping the goal of *Cities for People* at hand.

Jan's wonderful encouragement was a defining factor in my career, sparked by his never-ending confidence. Whether I was a graduate student, a young researcher, or an architect with Gehl Architects, Jan would always say, "We are sending the top-team; anything I can do, she can do better," which was of course entirely untrue since he said this about all of us, but it meant everything to me as a young professional coming into an overwhelming new situation somewhere in the world. Jan's finest gift was to make me feel qualified to address a crowd with professional confidence and with personal humility and humor. Today, almost 20 years after first meeting Jan Gehl, I still remember these important lessons.

As part of the strategy for making Copenhagen a greener and more people-friendly city, most major streets have now been changed from four-lane roads (left) into two-lane streets (right) to make room for bicycle lanes, street trees, and medians.

vision and a series of steps that progressively increase the level of commitment, and, most importantly, bring the city professionals and the city politicians along at every stage by showing them that people-city concepts work.

The Public Space Public Life surveys aim to make people and their use of public space visible and to place these issues at the forefront of urban planning. According to Jan, they "document the interplay between public life and public spaces…ensuring that people and public life are given the necessary attention in the city planning processes."[33]

Jan emphasizes the importance of cities having information on pedestrians and public life in just the same way as the traffic engineers invariably collect information on motor vehicle traffic and parking patterns. Information about pedestrians and use of public spaces was, at this time, not collected in any useful systematic way. Therefore, little information was generally available to planners about the users of public spaces. Jan reflects that "as the years have gone by, this has changed in quite a number of cities, such as Copenhagen and Melbourne. However, the majority of cities continue not to gather this type of information." This means that there is no documentation to assert the value of public spaces for people in debates with politicians, citizens, and traffic planners.

Jan's initial survey centered around three primary questions regarding how spaces are used:

What activities are occurring in the public realm?

Who is using the spaces and how?

How does the physical layout of buildings and public spaces influence activity patterns and the behavior of the individual users?[34]

As Jan said, it was not an "ambitious program." Rather, it recorded "everyday life, ordinary situations, and space in which daily life is lived," bringing this to the forefront of "attention and effort."[35]

Public Space Public Life surveys, as described in Jan's 2013 book *How to Study Public Life* (with Birgitte Svarre), focus on capturing a picture of "phenomena in constant flux," the life on the street.[36] As the authors explain "like the weather, life is difficult to predict. Nonetheless, meteorologists have developed methods enabling them to predict the weather."[37] One of the important findings from the early Copenhagen studies is that, actually, life is much more predictable than

Where small streets cross larger ones, sidewalks and bicycle lanes are routed across the small streets. Jan is quite happy about this solution because it enables his granddaughter Laura to walk to school without having to cross any streets.

most people would assume, that "every city has a rather constant daily rhythm."

The Public Space Public Life surveys, as they were later to be developed and refined, are made up of three parts:

Public space analysis: the quality and physical conditions of the public space frequently referred to as identifying the problems and potentials of a place. This includes surveys of the existing public space, pedestrian infrastructure, and the potential comfort and enjoyment of the pubic space (space quality). It also includes analysis of the traffic situations, conflicts between traffic and pedestrians, and how easy it is to walk through the city, along with the conditions for spending time in the public realm.

Public life analysis: the present use of public space, including surveys of pedestrian activity and staying activity levels in public places (space use) and characteristics of users of public space. This includes looking at the number of pedestrians, the number and duration of activities, how these levels change in different seasons and at different times of the day, week, and year.

Summary and recommendations: based on the analysis of the above, it seeks to answer "What can be done to improve the conditions for people in the city?"

The summary and recommendations were never part of the early studies, since the studies were purely academic and carried out to gain knowledge about how cities were used by people. Later, when the studies moved from being academic fact-finding missions to being part of the work of planning consultants, as with Gehl Architects, the recommendations were not only added, but became the purpose of the exercise.

THE 1995–1996 PUBLIC SPACE PUBLIC LIFE STUDY

In 1995, many years after the first series of studies in Copenhagen, Jan, Lars Gemzøe, and their team from the School of Architecture undertook a new, extensive Public Space Public Life study of Copenhagen. This survey was again conducted as an academic research project and was published in book form as *Public Space Public Life – Copenhagen, 1996*.[38] The book explains the improvements in Copenhagen up to 1995, starting with the closing of Strøget to cars in 1962.

The study highlights that Copenhagen was able to make this rather radical transition by

A program for widening the sidewalks has been put in place to improve conditions for the street life, allowing people to walk on the sunny side of the street.

The widening of the south-facing sidewalks is done with fine materials and detail, making room for a variety of people activities.

> *If it's monuments you're after in Copenhagen, don't look up. Look all around you, right there at street level. Our greatest monument is motion. It is a massive, constant, rhythmic, and life-sized legacy. The never-ending flow of Copenhageners on bicycles is like a symphony of human power, and it's been forty years in the making. There are few places in the world where the morning rush hour is graced with such poetic motion.*
>
> (City of Cyclists, Copenhagen Bicycle Life, City of Copenhagen 2009).

way of a very gradual, step-by-step process that slowly added to the public space within the city. This steady shift allowed time for the users of the city to adjust. During this time, the pedestrian areas had grown over six-fold from 15,800 m^2 to 95,750 m^2. The conversion of Strædet to a shared street in 1992 demonstrated a change from totally separating pedestrians from cars to mixing modes. The street was converted into a pedestrian-priority street, where all modes are welcome but pedestrians are the most important. Cars can use the street, but they must go very slowly and cannot drive down the full length of the road, which is broken up into short, one-way segments. Much of the street has café seating within the street space. This enables some vehicle access to shops but minimizes through traffic.

The public response to all the changes was very positive. Measures to reduce car traffic and improve access for pedestrians can be difficult to implement, even in Copenhagen, but once the improvements are seen, people are often pleased with the results. In Copenhagen, they concluded that the city center has become more attractive with each passing year while remaining less accessible to motorists. These two factors balance each other out completely, as the same number of people visit the city center now as 10 or 20 or 30 years ago."[39] The streets reached their full capacity very early on, and they are still going strong.

From all the changes, the surveys found that the number of people walking through the city was relatively stable (naturally, with some differences between winter and summer, but relatively similar to the 1968 survey. However, the number of people spending time in the city streets and squares had increased 3.5 times, the same as the increase in the area (square meters) set aside for pedestrian activities. Jan and Lars concluded that "every time Copenhagen has added another 14 m^2 for pedestrian use, a new person has come along and settled in to enjoy the city."[40]

In the years since 1988, international interest in the Copenhagen public life studies and their influence on the city's policies have

"Congratulations Copenhagen for being ranked as most livable city in the world". Noticeboard in the Copenhagen Metro celebrating the city's 2013 ranking by Monocle *magazine.*

Safety is crucial to establishing a bicycle culture. In Copenhagen, much work has been done to make bicycling safer, especially at intersections. Special signals and blue painted bicycle crossings are part of this strategy and have led to a steady increase in the use of bicycles. In 2015, the percentage of people bicycling to work or school reached 45%.

grown. First to ask for a similar study was Oslo, the capital of Norway. This study was carried out in 1988 as academic research and involved, for this same reason, no recommendations. The next city to ask for assistance was Stockholm, the Swedish capital. In 1990, this became the first private study Jan carried out as a consultant. This was also the first to include advice about what to do to create a more people-focused city. With these first international challenges, Jan continued as a researcher at the School of Architecture, gradually moving to a part-time position, and starting his own practice, Gehl Architects, in 2000 (presented in chapter 6).

THE 2005 PUBLIC SPACE PUBLIC LIFE STUDY OF COPENHAGEN

The 2005 surveys showed that the city center was increasingly a destination for recreational activities—to meet friends, to watch the world go by, to sightsee, or to sip coffee. The number of people present in the city center on a Sunday (a day when most stores are not open) increased by 78 percent between 1995 and 2005. The number of outdoor café seats increased by 47 percent. The city had 1,900 on-street parking spaces in 1995 and 1,520 in 2005, a 20-percent reduction. This reduction occurred even though the car-ownership rates amongst city residents, between 1999 and 2004, increased by 11 percent.

This study was conducted in collaboration with the City, and had widespread support from tourist, business, and cultural organizations. And for the first time, it included surveys not only in the city center but in all parts of the city.

After the 2005 survey, Public Space Public Life surveys became a part of the City of Copenhagen's municipal routine, the same way that traffic surveys are undertaken. For Jan this is "a victory in the battle of ideas and in the battle for city spending." He believes that all cities should undertake public life surveys just as cities always survey how cars use the city.

By 2005, the City of Copenhagen had undergone some major infrastructure projects, including: the building of the Øresundsbroen (Oresund Bridge), which connects Copenhagen to Malmö, Sweden, through a 16 kilometer tunnel and bridge; the opening of the first metro line (in 2002); and the opening of a new waterfront area with the creation of a large Opera House in 2004. Furthermore, along with these big changes, the city had continued to expand cycling facilities and to further increase the amount of public space. Since the initial conversion of Strøget to a pedestrian street in 1962, the pedestrian-only and pedestrian-priority network had been gradually expanded in the city center and many new squares and parks in the surrounding residential areas were created.

A number of planning documents for the city, such as "Metropolis for People: Visions and Goals for Urban Life in Copenhagen 2015" (2009), reflect the huge influence Jan has had on Copenhagen. This general influence on mindsets is also reflected in the latest Danish National Architectural Policy, revised in 2014 under the new heading "Putting People First. Metropolis for People." It states that Copenhagen should be the "best city for people in the world."[43] The policy sets out the rationale for the need for increased public life within the city, how the City of Copenhagen will create better public spaces, and how they will encourage people to use these spaces. The policy also sets out how it will measure the changes in space and use. Since 2009, the policy has been followed up by a number of supporting documents, including a best-practice guide in 2011. The results of the policy are monitored in a biannual "Urban Life Account," looking at trends in urban life and use of public space. This report measures how many people are walking within the city, how safe and happy they feel walking, the use of public spaces (particularly how long people stay within them), and other urban quality measures. The 2013 report also provides an exploration of the use of the city from a child's perspective.[44]

What started in 1966 as curiosity concerning how people used public spaces has, over time, developed into both city policies and Danish national policies centered on "putting people first,"; and Copenhagen has been the laboratory in which to study a more people-centered approach.

SUMMING UP

This period in Jan's professional life continued the use of Copenhagen as a laboratory, a testing ground, for formalizing and mainstreaming his methodologies and for bringing people into public space design with the formation of the Public Space Public Life surveys. This period also saw Jan's transition from academia to consultancy. His surveys provided evidence that people want to be part of public space in cities and that the politics of creating people-focused cities are important for their livability, sustainability, and health.

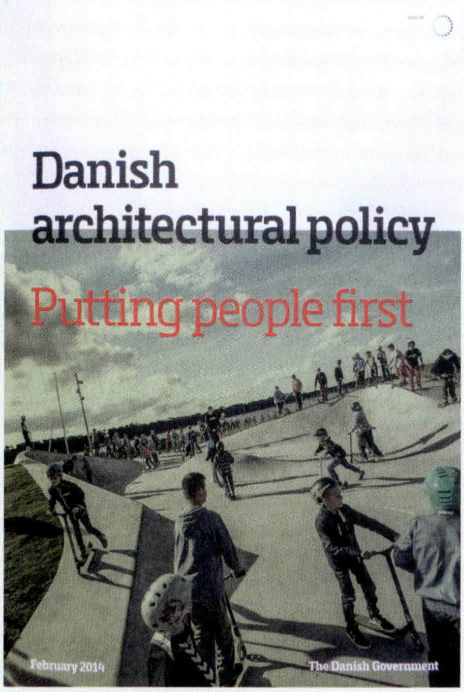

For 50 years, people-oriented architecture and city planning have been researched, documented, and discussed. This mindset has, by now, been firmly established in Copenhagen and in all of Denmark.
Above left: The Danish national architecture policy was revised in 2015 under a new heading: "Putting people first."
Above right: Marianne Jelved, Danish Minister of Culture (2011–2015), reading one of her favorite books. (From the ministry's website)
Below: New Danish ministers arrive by bike to the Royal Castle to be commissioned by the Queen in 2011.

JAN GEHL'S INFLUENCE ON COPENHAGEN

by Klaus Bondam, former Mayor for City Planning (2006–2009), City of Copenhagen

I moved to Copenhagen right after high school, back in 1992. At that time, Copenhagen was a shabby city: poor, inactive, dirty, and not very attractive. The inhabitants were mainly old people—those who never had the money to move out—and a lot of students who couldn't wait until they could afford to move out. Then something started to change. I personally believed that it was in 1996 when Copenhagen was European Capital of Culture. Suddenly, we started to understand what a gem of a city we lived in, and how we could use our public spaces for activities, events, people-watching, and all kinds of other nice urban stuff. We took in the streets and squares. At that time, I fell in love with my city. I, along with many other young people in my generation, decided to stay in the city, not doing like our parents who had moved out to the suburbs. I started my professional career and established my family in the city. As most urban young people in my generation, I couldn't afford a car (which are luckily heavily taxed in Denmark). I cycled around the city. I realised that the real treasure in our city was that we slowly had created an urban life where we could see, meet, and talk to other people eye-to-eye. I realized that this gave a vibrant feel to our city while creating a feeling of safety because of the amount of people present in the streetscape at most times during the day. We had succeeded through our actions to create a city in which people were not hidden behind car windows, where you sensed the seasons, and where most people were physically active walking or biking every day.

In 2002, I was elected to the City Council, and in 2006, I was appointed to be Mayor for City Planning, a post that I held for four years. Copenhagen hosted the UN Climate Summit COP15 in 2009, and the time leading up to the COP was a good time to shape up some of our city policies on environmental issues, including urban life and liveability. Being married to a landscape architect, I was aware of Jan Gehl and his studies of street life. I also knew that some of the 'real' building architects were not that crazy about Jan Gehl's ongoing talks on life between the buildings. This didn't correspond very well with the aesthetics, clear and sharp lines, and rationality of the modernist architects of the welfare state. All this nonsense about people and their impulsive behavior—and the urban life it contributed to—didn't fit into their plans.

Having an artistic background myself, being trained as an actor, I actually liked this focus on people. For me, the spontaneous happiness and well-being of people in the city is essential in policy making. I therefore invited Jan Gehl

to City Hall, and we clicked right away. Here was a man who had the same interest in and love for the behavior of the human being. He shared my belief that if we can see and meet each other, we create a platform for engagement, integration—and also innovation. The City of Copenhagen invited Jan Gehl and Gehl Architects to be our consultant on a new—and to my knowledge the city's first—policy on urban life and liveability in Copenhagen. It was named Metropolis for People and was accepted by the City Council in 2009.

It has three themes: 'More urban life for all', 'More people to walk more,' and 'More people to stay longer.' The idea was to "prioritize daily urban life while, at the same time, creating the possibility for the secret, the eccentric, and the temporary to flourish. For these reasons, we want to create more urban life for everybody with a variety of urban space and activities twenty-four hours a day all year round." We realized that "some urban life is governed by necessity. We have to do the shopping, fetch the children, go to and from work irrespective of how the city is laid out and equipped. All the fun things, recreational life in the city, the experiences and our personal enjoyment and expressions will only happen if it is a pleasurable place to be. For this reason, we want to create squares, parks, streets, and waterside quays which invite more people to stay there longer—both in the city center, in new urban areas as well as where we live and go around on a daily basis."

We set up tangible targets that were measured every year and used as an inspiration for new initiatives.

Metropolis for People and Jan Gehl's deep involvement in new urban policies in Copenhagen have taken our city to a new level, serving as an example of how a future sustainable and people-centered development isn't a contradiction to economic growth; an example that many cities worldwide are inspired by today.

Thanks to Jan Gehl—and Gehl Architects—the question and challenges of creating good urban life is integrated completely in all relevant Copenhagen policies today.

And I feel lucky to have good cooperation and dialogue with Jan Gehl in my present position as CEO of Danish Cyclists' Federation. Jan Gehl is, like myself, a dedicated cyclist—and Gehl Architects is also a cherished and internationally known member of the Cycling Embassy of Denmark. Cycling in a safe, secure, and well-constructed bicycle-friendly environment is, of course, an essential part of a good, sustainable urban life . . . a city for people.

For years, congestion on the bicycle lanes has been a major problem in Copenhagen. Many steps have been taken to relieve this problem. Many bicycle lanes have been widened and new "relief" bicycle ways, through parks and disused railway lines, have been made to supplement the bicycle lanes. The only problem worse than having too many bicyclists is having too many cars.

Robinhood
loves

5

CHANGING MINDSETS

CHANGING MINDSETS

"Jan's path-breaking work on public spaces, urban liveability, and sociability of cities stands at the forefront of contemporary thinking about cities, and his expansive contributions in the form of projects and policy guidelines for streetscapes and neighborhoods serve as inspiration and point of departure for many around the globe."

—Diane Davis, Chair, Department of Urban Planning and Design, Graduate School of Design, Harvard University, 2016

During his long career, Jan has been involved in a number of very different types of activities, from research to teaching to consultancy. Jan is often asked which of his activities he feels has mattered most. Is it the 40 years of teaching countless students in Copenhagen and around the world? Is it the lectures and presentations to universities, professional institutes, conferences, and public meetings across the globe? Is it the magazine articles, interviews, radio, television, and film documentaries? Or perhaps it is the work in cities where he applied his research to real-life projects?

All these activities have been important to Jan and contributed to changing the mindsets of students, professionals, and politicians, but he will never hesitate to point out that of all the activities he has been involved in, his six books matter to him the most. From *Life Between Buildings* in 1971 to his latest book *How to Study Public Life* in 2013, the books have gradually expanded and deepened as more research, experience, and examples from cities worldwide have been accumulated and integrated into the overall story on how to practice people-oriented architecture and planning. The books also illustrate a timeline of hope, as more and more examples of cities returning to humanistic design are added.

The books are characterized by simple, straightforward language and the careful integration of text and illustrations. Not a single photo is included that does not "plainly tell the story." This format has generally proven to make the books easily understood by audiences far beyond academic circles and in many different cultures. The books illustrate and communicate complex human behaviors and the results of urban planning decisions clearly and easily, and often with a gentle humor.

The books serve different purposes. Some like *Life Between Buildings* and *Cities for People* deal with basic research on how life in public spaces is influenced by the physical environment. Others such as *New City Spaces* and *New City Life* deal with how public spaces and public life are evolving as society changes. The book *Public Spaces – Public Life, Copenhagen 1996* tells the story of how spaces and public life in Copenhagen developed in the period between 1962 and 1996 and presents the methods on how to study public life in a modern city. This subject is further updated and enlarged into a toolkit in Jan's most recent book, *How to Study Public Life*, in which the methods developed over the entire course of the research decades are explained and placed in the wider context of methods to study how people interact with the built environment.

Together, the six books tell the story of a developing idea and its application to changing our physical built environment. They constitute a legacy. The books have been met with an unusual worldwide interest. Ever since *Life Between Buildings* was translated into English in 1987, all the books, especially the two presenting the basic research, have spread far and wide across the world.

Altogether, Jan's books have been published in more than 35 languages, and they are still coming out in new corners of the world. An estimated 200,000 volumes of Jan's books are out there.

> *"I was always more interested in changing the mindset. Someone else can change the cities."*
>
> —Jan Gehl[45]

Teamwork

Life Between Buildings was written by Jan alone, but all of the subsequent books have been developed in teams, which is much more in tune with Jan's temperament and style of working. Foremost in his team is architect Lars Gemzøe who joined the urban design department of the Royal Danish Academy of Fine Arts as a lecturer in 1978 and who became a close research associate and co-author for the books to follow.

Lars Gemzøe.

Book team for New City Life: *Sia Kirknæs and Britt Søndergaard flanked by Jan Gehl and Lars Gemzøe.*

In 2006 *New City Life* was developed by Jan and Lars as part of their work at the Center for Public Space Research, along with architects Sia Kirknæs and Britt Søndergaard.

Cities for People has only Jan's name on the cover, but inside this cover we find an experienced team of helpers. On the day of publishing the Danish version, the team gathered in front of the Danish Architecture Centre for a team photo shown on page 97.

How to Study Public Life was developed in close cooperation with Birgitte Svarre who brought, as background, a degree in modern culture from the University of Copenhagen and a PhD in urban design from the School of Architecture to the team effort.

Birgitte Svarre and Jan Gehl.

LIFE BETWEEN BUILDINGS 1971, 1987, 2011

Jan Gehl

Life Between Buildings (*Livet mellem husene*) was published in Danish in 1971 by the School of Architecture in Copenhagen. In today's language, it would have been described as a PhD dissertation. But in those days, it was a book summing up four years of research conducted by Jan on the use of outdoor spaces in cities and residential areas.

It was a small, compact paperback book with 100 pages of text and 100 pages of illustrations. The cover was a photo depicting a rather 1970'ish scene—a festive street party.

The book looks at life between buildings, in which public space activity is introduced and examples are presented to show how public life is greatly influenced by the physical environment. This is followed by an overview of how this life has been faring in various historic periods leading into a heavy criticism of modernist planning principles as effectively discouraging, or rather preventing, life between buildings. The next part of the book looks at the art of making streets, referring to the art of city making that had been discarded by modernists, and had to be rediscovered. The book goes on to describe, in detail, some preconditions for such art—predominantly an understanding of how our senses work—and continues by reversing a number of modernist planning principles such as concentrate instead of disperse and integrate instead of segregate. All of these principles are related to city and site planning. But Jan also underlines that the treatment of the people scale is extremely important—the battle for urban quality has to be won (or lost) at the human scale. Good conditions for walking, standing, sitting, seeing, hearing, and so on must be provided. As a final conclusion, the book emphasizes the importance of the social dimension in architecture, the understanding that whenever we build anything we influence social patterns.

With the perspective of some 45 years, the original book can be seen as predominantly a critique of modernism and a debate about

> *.......thoughtful, beautiful and enlightening...*
>
> Jane Jacobs, on *Life Between Buildings*

> *...over the years Jan Gehl's message has been developed with increased concentration and here achieves the characteristic of timeless truth...*
>
> Ralph Erskine, 1987
> (From the foreword to the English version)

1971 original version in Danish

1987 revised edition and the first version in English

2011 seventh edition republished in the United States by Island Press

The three different types of public life introduced in Life Between Buildings*: necessary activities, optional activities, and social activities.*

The connection between city quality and types of activities was presented in a graph illustrating how the important optional and social activities are very dependent on good quality in the people landscape.

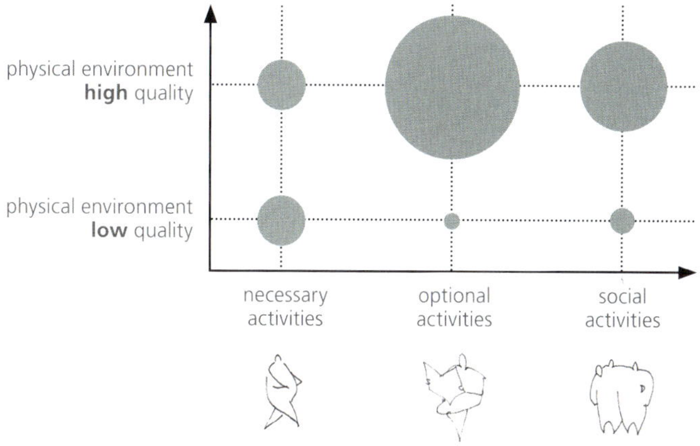

the shortcomings of this planning ideology as seen through the eyes of the people who actually used these projects. This book introduced human life between buildings as an important issue that most certainly needed to be looked after.

Compared with PhD dissertations today, *Life Between Buildings* demonstrates a very different approach. There are almost no references to other researchers or other viewpoints, partly because there was not much to refer to at this point in time and partly because this was not the way this piece of research was conducted. The book is almost solely based on Jan's own observations and reflections. By way of research, it is the work of an autodidact, an architect trained in observations but not in research methodology. This also reflects the lack of research tradition at this early stage in architecture research.

In 1971 when *Life Between Buildings* was published, discussions about quality of the built environment were starting to gain momentum, and the book was immediately very popular in Denmark. Over a rather short period, some 10,000 copies of this book were distributed among Danish readers, showing that the interest reached far beyond the academic and professional circles. As Jan reflects, "If the book had only been sold to architects,

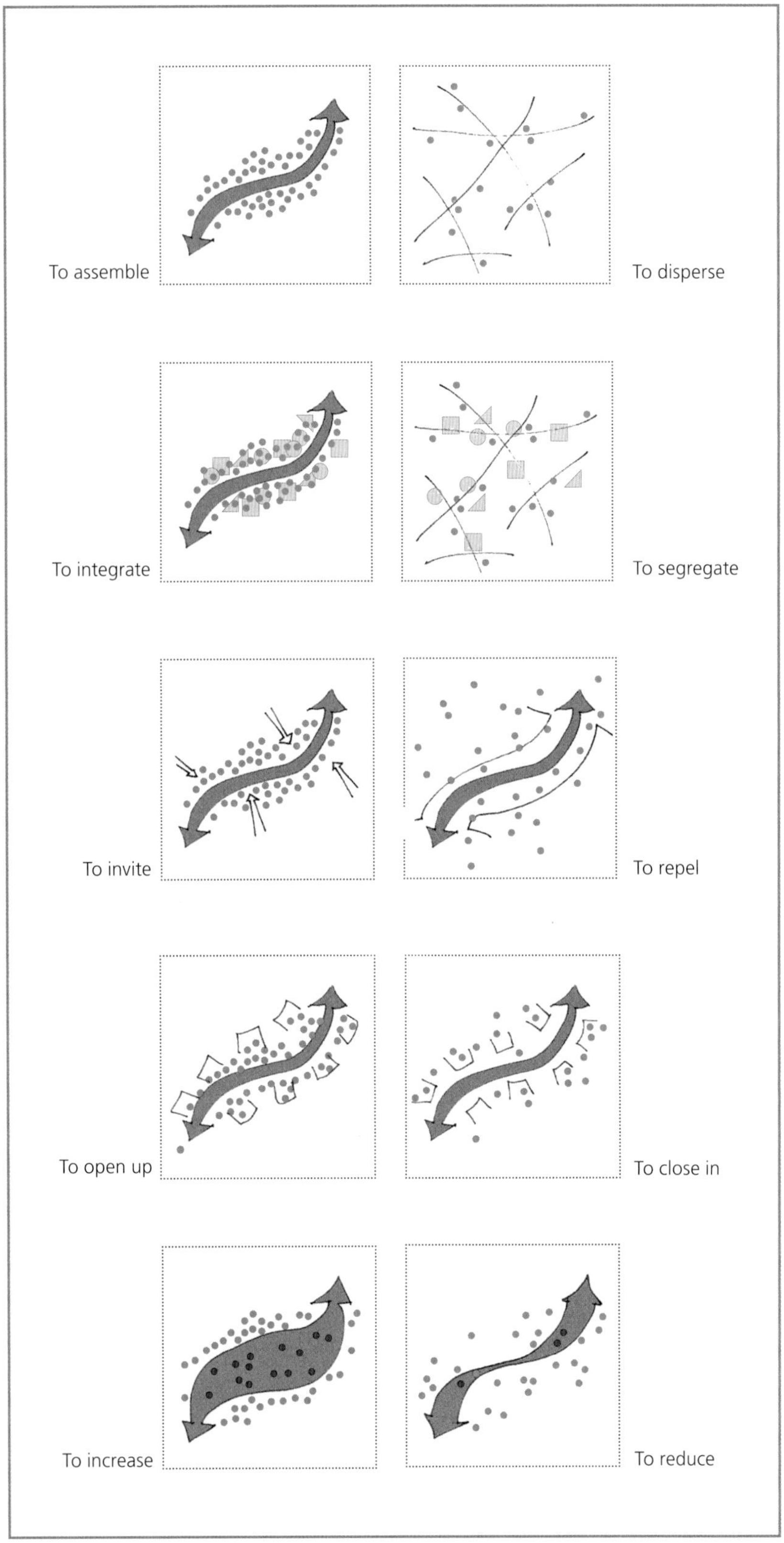

Key illustration from Life Between Buildings *showing important conditions for strengthening the life between buildings. In the left column are all the things one should consider. In the right column are planning principles that would generally deter life between buildings. By and large, the right column describes the main principles used in modernist planning.*

each Danish architect at that point would have been the happy owner of four copies!"

"Life between buildings" quickly became a common phrase in Denmark. In project descriptions, in competition programs, in municipal policies, and in many other places you now see the phrase appear without further explanation. This reflected the strong, but at first rather local, success.

After publishing *Life Between Buildings* (and Ingrid's simultaneous publishing of *Living Environment*), Ingrid and Jan went to Toronto for a year and lectured on these two newly published Danish books. Here they found, to their great surprise, that this people-oriented approach to housing and planning was seen as something very new and very progressive in this part of the world. But there was still not an English translation of either book at this point. Instead, *Life Between Buildings* was published in 1978 in Dutch, and in 1980, a Norwegian version was launched together with an update of the Danish version. For 16 years, it was a North-European phenomenon, with the book known in Denmark, Holland, and Norway only. It seemed to touch a nerve with the Dutch Woonerf movement and traffic-calming schemes and influenced a number of new town developments in Sweden and Holland.

Already in this 1980 update, the book started to change from being predominantly a book for debate and a critique of modernism into more of a handbook. The "art of making

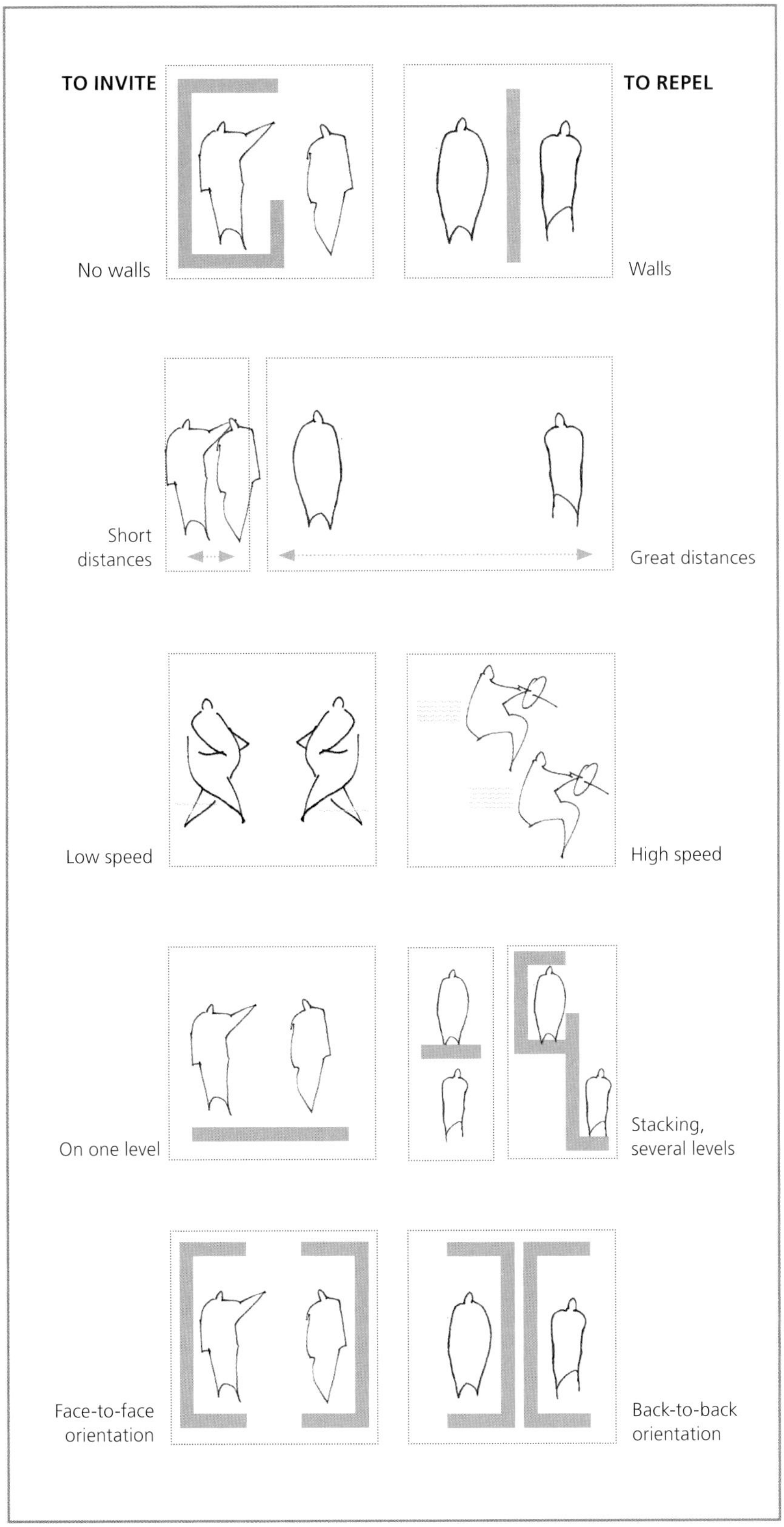

Discussion concerning the relations between built form and the human senses plays an important role in the book. The left column shows circumstances and details that may invite human interaction. The right column shows circumstances that will prevent contact. By and large, the right column describes the situation in many suburban areas.

streets" headline disappeared as it was not needed anymore since this concept was, by then, generally accepted. Where the message of the original book was "life between buildings is mistreated and should be taken care of," the message from the 1980 version, and the versions thereafter became "life between buildings is important and this is what we should do."

In 1987, 16 years after the original publication in Danish, *Life Between Buildings* was finally published in English by Van Nostrand Reinhold in New York. The English-language edition was based on the 1980 Danish version, but the illustrations and examples from Italy and Scandinavia were supplemented with other international examples. This US publication, according to Jan, "did not have a very long and glorious life." Not much was being done to market it, and after three print runs, the book went out of print sometime in the 1990s. However, the English-language edition was translated into a variety of other languages including Japanese, Italian, and Chinese in the early 1990s.

In 1996, 25 years after its first publication, *Life Between Buildings* was once again updated and published in its third Danish edition. At the same time, the Danish Architectural Press took over the publication of the English version. A second English-language edition was launched and the international marketing intensified. In the coming years, 1998 to 2007, the fourth, fifth, and sixth versions in Danish and English were published. By the sixth edition the illustrations were adapted to the twenty-first century, removing the few remaining "1970s photos of longhaired youngsters in sheepskin coats," making room for more current examples. The foreword to all these versions stated laconically that the basic message was unchanged—*look after the people*. Jan has said on several occasions that after even 30 or 40 years, he found very few items in the general text and messages that needed to be changed. "From the first instance, this book was about the interaction between Homo sapiens and the built environment. And 40 years later, it still is Homo sapiens and nothing much has changed there. He or she is still standing in the niches enjoying looking at other people as was the case back in the 1960s."

What changed after this span of years was the international interest in this book. After 20 years, it had become a classic globally. From 1996 to 2016, *Life Between Buildings* was translated into 20 languages. Jan elaborates that "apart from versions in exotic places like Vietnam, Bangladesh, and Iran, major languages like Russian and German were included in this batch." Reprintings were organized in Italy and Japan, and by 2011, some 40 years later, the book came back to the US to be reprinted in a seventh edition by Island Press.

Life Between Buildings is still available in most places, and continues to be published in new languages; Turkish and Icelandic may be next.

The story about *Life Between Buildings* is one of a book with a simple message that grew out of a series of modest studies but addressed some universally felt problems. This could explain the wide movement and longevity of the book—from the beginning, it has been a simple message about Homo sapiens and the urban environment. The history of this book shows how this simple message has increasingly become a universal concern.

In 2006, Life Between Buildings *was published in Bangladesh. Ruhan Shama, from the NGO WBB (Working for a Better Bangladesh), was a key person in organizing this version.*

As times go by

Life Between Buildings *has been published in many versions and over a period of more than four decades. Over time, the cover has subtly changed, reflecting changes in various societies and the shifting focus of architecture and city planning. The cover of the 1971 edition was wild and local. The 1980 cover became more civilized, and hinted at an interest in village architecture and "the good old days." By 1987, the growing focus on cities and city life became more evident. Since 1996, the editions have become increasingly international and expressing life in general.*

1971

1980

1987

1996–2011...

1971

DENMARK

1978

NETHERLAND

1980

NORWAY

1987

USA

1990
1991
1992

JAPAN

ITALY

CHINA

1996
1997

TAIWAN

COSTA RICA

2000
2002
2003

CZECH REP.

CHINA

KOREA

2006
2008

SPAIN

BANGLADESH

VIETNAM

2011
2012
2013
2014

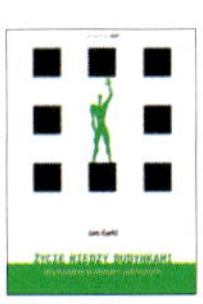

POLAND

SERBIA

ROMANIA

IRAN

RUSSIA

GERMANY

JAPAN 2

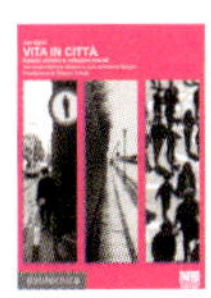

ITALY 2

USA 7

THAILAND

GREECE

The barcode from Life Between Buildings *displayed in neon lights in a temporary art installation in Sydney in 2009–10. (Artists D. Hadley, H. Tribe, and Maix Mayer)*

Printing history by 2016

In 45 years, Life Between Buildings *has been published in several editions and in many languages. It is interesting that for the first 16 years, the book was a local, north-European phenomenon. In 1987, the first English edition was published in New York. Since then, the book has been published in many other parts of the world. In fact, most editions have been published since 2000, showing a steep increase in the interest in the subject.*

PUBLIC SPACE PUBLIC LIFE – COPENHAGEN, 1996

Jan Gehl & Lars Gemzøe

In 1996, the City of Copenhagen was selected as the European Capital of Culture by the European Union. Just as was done in the many previous "capitals," the local institutions contemplated how they could contribute to this celebration. In the School of Architecture, it was decided that they would strengthen the already existing collaboration between the School of Architecture and the City by having the city life researchers from the urban design department carry out another, and considerably enlarged, Public Space Public Life study. This is how the study and book *Public Spaces Public Life, Copenhagen 1996* came about. The school of architecture, the City of Copenhagen, the business community of central Copenhagen, and various foundations all contributed to cover the costs. The studies were carried out during 1995, in order to be ready for 1996.

The study and the book are organized in three parts. Part one is an overview of the spaces available in the city, presenting the history of how the car-free public spaces within the city had developed since 1962. The city center in 1996 is described—residences, educational institutions, night life, safety, traffic, parking, bicycling, and many other items related to the present state of the city. The second part of the book presents the current use of the city through summer and winter, on the main streets and on the side streets, during events and ordinary days as well as the impact of street vendors and performers and the rapid growth in the café culture. While the observation methods used were originally developed for the studies recorded in *Life Between Buildings,* the third part of the book introduces a new study tool: the interview. Not having previous experience in this technique, Jan and Lars asked professor David Yencken from the University of Melbourne to join the team and organize the interviews. These interviews cast valuable light on a number of questions that the observations alone could not answer: Who were the city users? Where did they come from? How did they travel to and from the city? What were their motives for coming? What did they like and dislike about the city? This was seen as a most valuable expansion of the traditional counting and observation studies.

A characteristic of this book is the presentation of maps, plans, and graphics that tell the story of the city, how the users of the public spaces conduct their public lives, and how study methodologies were applied. In Copenhagen, the book was celebrated as an illustration of how the city had developed.

Development of car-free streets and squares, 1962–1996

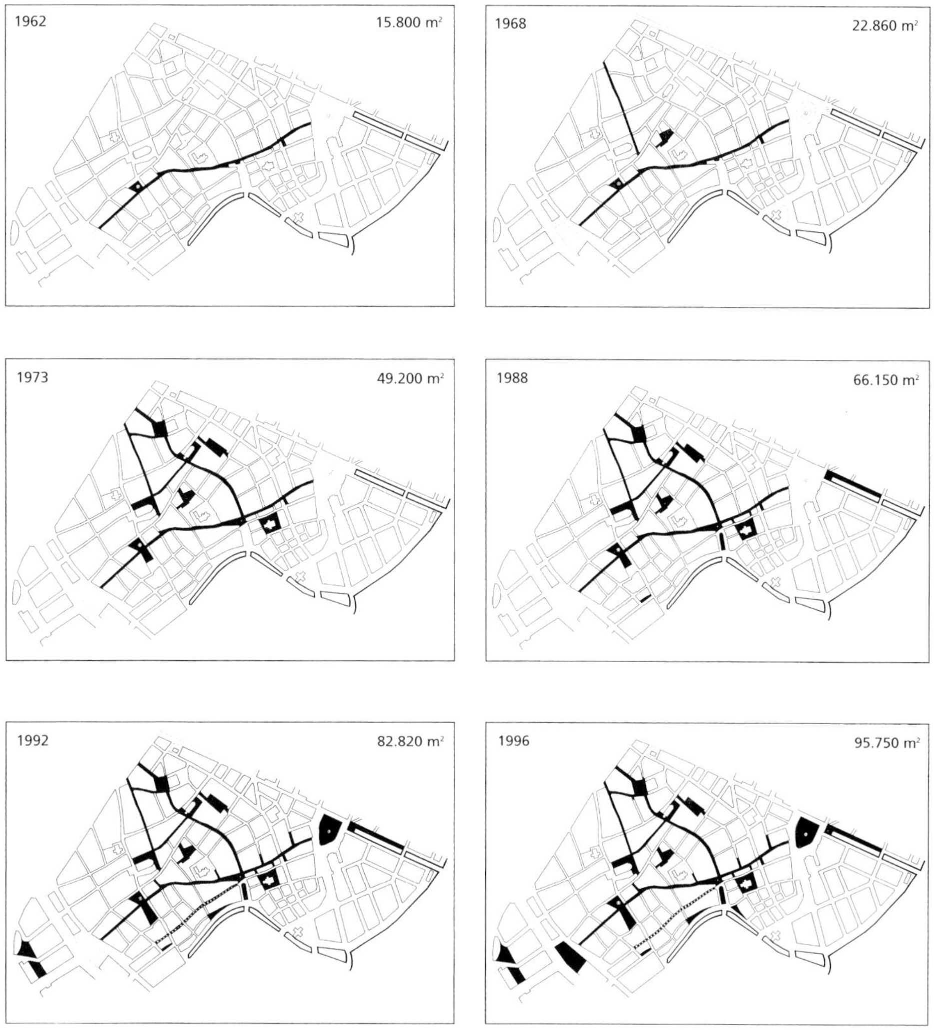

The main focus of the book Public Spaces Public Life–Copenhagen 1996 *was to describe the impressive development of the people landscape in central Copenhagen from 1962 to 1996. Above is shown how the car free areas were expanded in this period. By 1995, there was seven times more space for people in the city. ca 1:29.000*

An English-language version was produced by the Danish Architectural Press. Though the book is about Copenhagen, this English-language version had a much larger distribution than the Danish version. Ten years after the last Danish book was printed and sold, the English version was still being published and sold, emphasizing a great interest particularly in the methodologies used and the results achieved well beyond Copenhagen.

From 1962 to 1995, the average number of people spending time in the city tripled (during afternoon hours on summer weekdays). As more and more space was freed of cars, more and more people came and used the spaces. Throughout the period, it was determined that for every 13 extra square meters provided, one extra person was found to be present, lingering in the city.

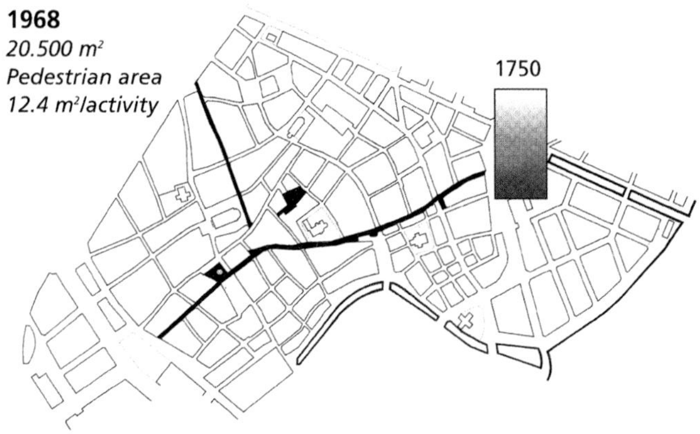

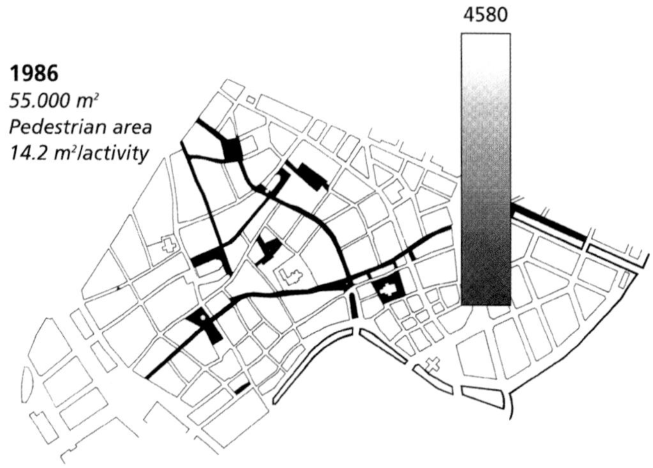

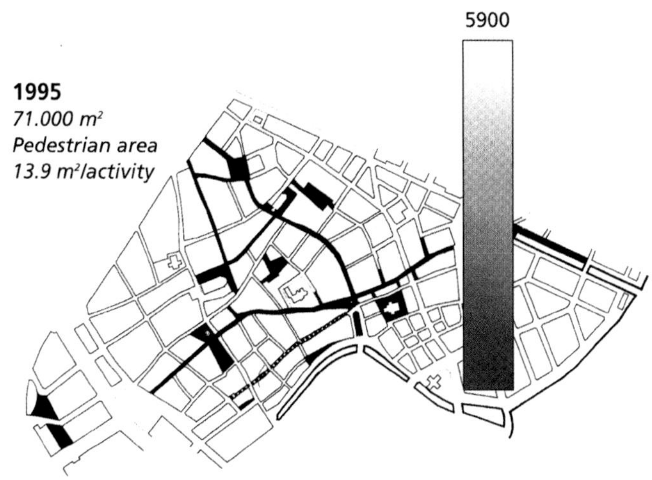

ca 1:23.000

In 1992, the first pedestrian-priority street was introduced. Strædet, a street running parallel to the main street Strøget, has café chairs, pedestrians, bicyclists, and a few slow-moving cars sharing the street space and has become one of the most pleasant streets in the city.

NEW CITY SPACES, 2000

Jan Gehl & Lars Gemzøe

Nicknamed "The Hardware Book", *New City Spaces* is different from most of Jan's other writings, because it is a book not about life but about built form. It is an architecture book about "new" public spaces from the final decades before the turn of the century. The reason for producing this book was to meet the growing demand for useable text-books on contemporary public spaces. During this time, many architecturally interesting streets and squares were being built all over the world. Together with Lars Gemzøe, Jan set about documenting what was happening in the area of public space design in the final years of the twentieth century.

The book is divided into three parts, starting with a chapter called "Winning Back Public Space." This chapter presents four distinctly different types of cities found at this point in time: the Traditional City, the Invaded City, the Abandoned City, and the Reconquered City. The traditional city was a city dominated by pedestrians and public life, whereas, in the invaded city, the city was dominated by automobiles with people and public life pushed aside. In the abandoned city, people had given up altogether and had left the public spaces. It was a city completely empty of people. The reconquered city was a new phenomenon at this time. It was a city

The traditional city.

The invaded city.

The abandoned city.

The reconquered city.

In New City Spaces *four different types of cities are discussed, ranging from the old, traditional cities to the more recent, reconquered cities that emerge once the car invasion has been addressed.*

where the cars were being pushed aside and the public spaces were being given back to people. The public spaces that helped to facilitate this were the main focus of the rest of the book.

The second part of the book presents nine cities—reconquered in various degrees. There are five European cities: Barcelona, Lyon, Strasbourg, Freiburg, and Copenhagen and four cities in other parts of the world: Portland, Oregon, in North America; Curitiba, Brazil, and Cordoba, Argentina, in South America; and Melbourne, in Australia. The book describes what had been done to "reconquer" these cities, how these processes came about, and what could now be seen and enjoyed within their public spaces. The cities were chosen deliberately. There are both old historic cities and newer cities, proving that "reconquering cities is not an exercise reserved for cozy, old historic centers, but is needed and can be carried out in all types of urban centers."

The third part of the book presents 39 architecturally interesting streets and squares from all corners of the world. One criterion for the selection was that the construction or reconstruction of these public spaces happened in the period 1985–2000, which was the period when the interest in public life and public spaces really started to be renewed

Case study: Strasbourg, France

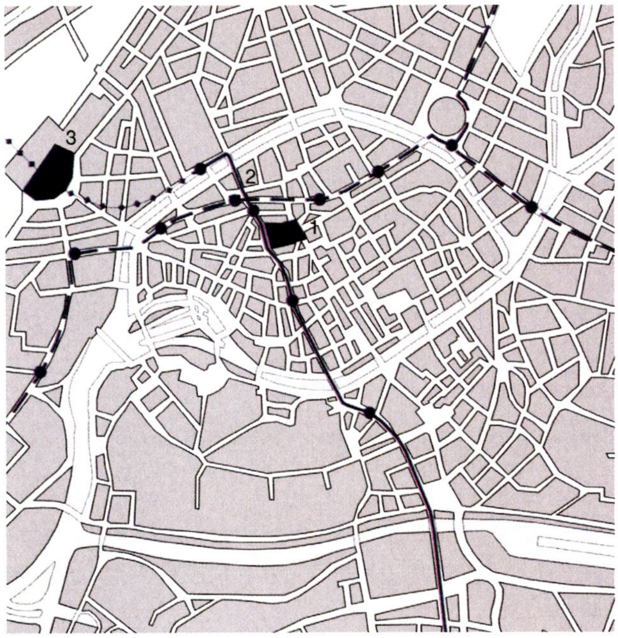

Nine reconquered cities are presented in the book. For each city, important aspects of the strategy are presented together with photos and a brief story of the improvement process. Above are excerpts from the description of Strasbourg in France.

Case study: Pioneer Courthouse Square, Portland, USA

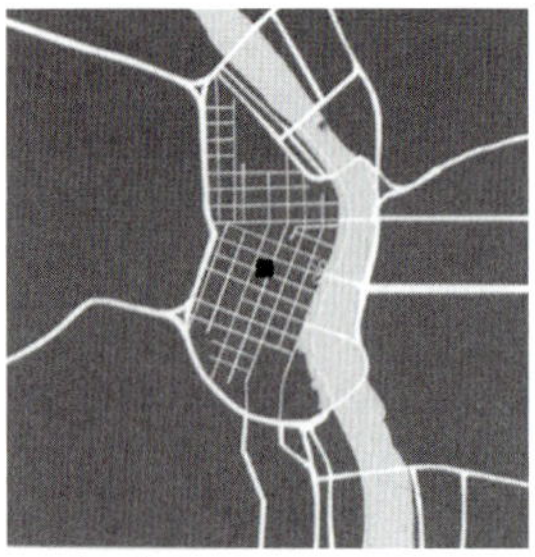

Portland, Oregon
1:100.000

Pioneer Courthouse Square
1:5.000

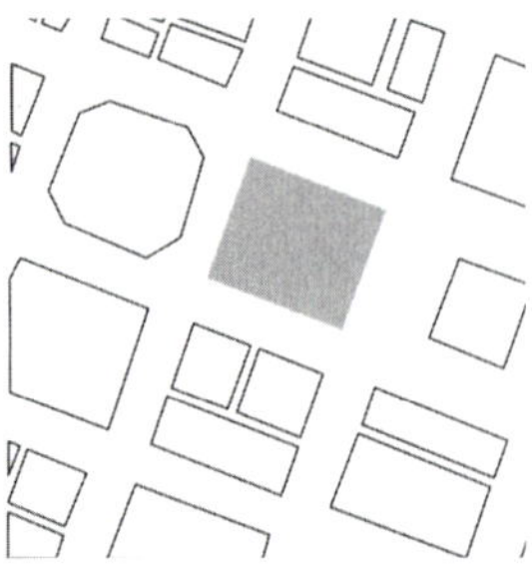

Central pedestrian zone: 5.100 m^2
1:5.000

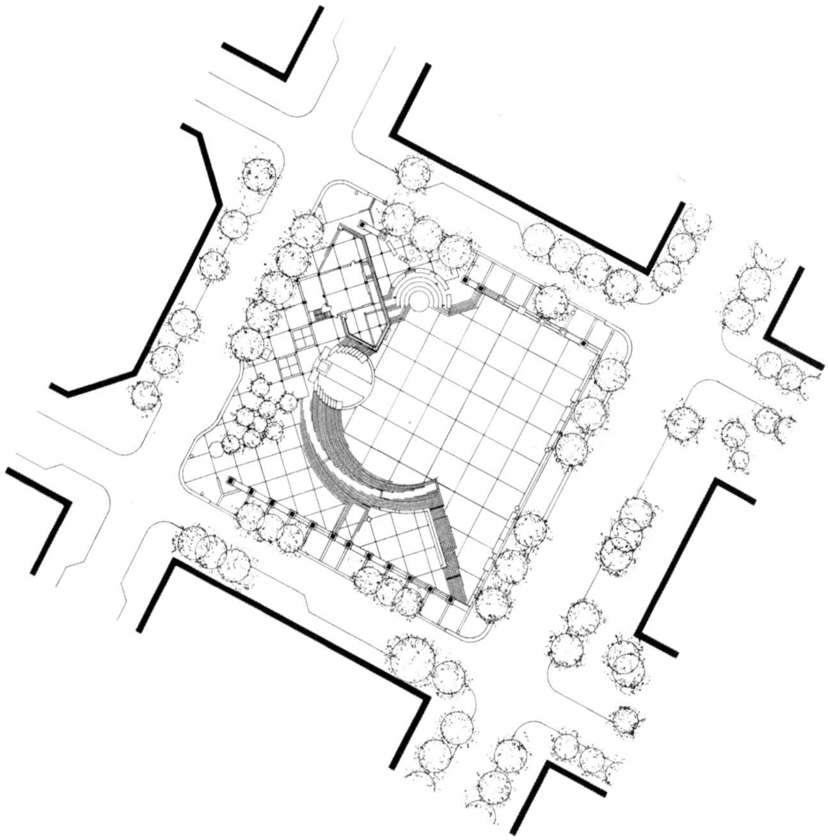

In the second part of the book, 39 architecturally interesting streets and squares from the last decades of the twentieth century are presented, each with maps and plans showing location, the immediate surroundings, and the actual project. The public spaces presented are from all parts of the world. Shown as examples are excerpts from the presentation of Pioneer Courthouse Square in Portland, Oregon, USA.

worldwide. Another criterion for selection was the principle that all spaces (and cities) needed to have been visited and evaluated by Lars and Jan. This was to guard against architectural hype. As Jan said, "Actually, some places told about were found to be not that exciting, others looked much better in the architecture magazines than in real life, and one square in Switzerland was even found not to exist anymore. Somebody had torn it down." Altogether, Jan and Lars found strong arguments for personally seeing everything before it went into the book.

The collection of public spaces is wide ranging—from the rebuilt Champs-Elysees in Paris through to a series of new squares in Barcelona and Lyon and to a number of humble, but architecturally interesting, public spaces found in towns and villages in various corners of the world. From the start until publication, the process of identifying the cities and spaces, of visiting and selecting the ones to be included, and of preparing the graphics took eight years.

In the fall of 2000, the book was finally ready for publication, in Danish and English, by the Danish Architectural Press, which had handled Jan's previous books. The publishing event hosted by the School of Architecture was turned into a major celebration with the Danish Minister of Cities Jytte Andersen and the American Ambassador to Denmark, Architect Richard D. Swett, launching the two versions. Pointing to the cover photo from Portland, the Ambassador was especially happy. "Obviously, you Europeans really appreciate US architecture," he said.

Throughout its lifespan, the English version was distributed from Denmark, which may not have been the most efficient way of spreading the word, but it worked sufficiently enough to see the book published in a number of other languages. In the early years of the 2000s, the book was published in Czech, Spanish, Portuguese, and Chinese followed in 2012 by a Russian version published by the City of Moscow.

Printing History

Danish

English

Portuguese

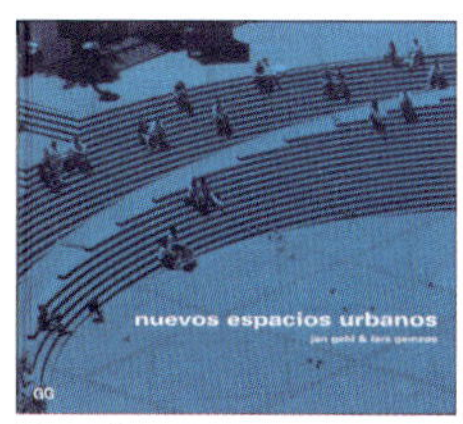

Spanish

Chinese

Czech

Russian

Essentially a textbook on general architecture, New City Spaces *has been published in several languages following the original Danish and English editions.*

NEW CITY LIFE, 2006

Jan Gehl, Lars Gemzøe, Sia Kirknæs & Britt Søndergaard

A quick look at the front cover of *New City Life* tells the story of this book: there are some drastic new changes happening to the way public spaces are used. The photo is from an early 2005 spring day in a square in a Copenhagen residential district and shows how the city spaces were being intensely used, almost like a park, for recreation and enjoyment. New ways of using public spaces were (and are still) fast developing. *New City Life* describes these emerging patterns. The book was published by the Danish Architectural Press in Danish and English editions.

New City Life was, right from the start, nicknamed "The Software Book." It builds on the description of the renewed celebration of public spaces introduced in the previous book, *New City Spaces.* Copenhagen is once again the focus, but this time it is not only the public life in the central districts of the city that are studied and presented. Rather, it is a cross section through the entire city, from the outlying districts to the squares in front of the Town Hall and the Royal Castle. The book describes the changes in the use of public space from the center to the periphery of Copenhagen over the full year of 2005.

The framework for this study was the Center for Public Space Research, which had been in operation for a number of years and was given a major lift in 2003 through funding from Realdania, as described in chapter 4. The *New City Life* investigation became one of the main enterprises carried out at this time by the center. Where all previous studies were carried out as "sideshows to the daily urban design teachings," the funding enabled the authors to "devote their energies to this study and the tools necessary for conducting and communicating the tale." The center also made it possible to expand the study team. Architects Sia Kirknæs and Britt S. Søndergaard, both fresh from studies at the urban design department, joined as researchers and authors.

This book is presented in two parts. The first part is a general description of the evolution from necessary activities within public space, such as walking to work, to the more and more frequent optional activities such as sitting and watching the world go by. This development, and its changing demands on the quality of the public spaces, are described in several ways, including a diagram Jan often uses called The Whale. The changes in the use patterns of city spaces led to the realization that the quality of the spaces was a major precondition for any optional recreational activities. Only where spaces of good quality were offered would urban dwellers of the "leisure-time society" consider using them.

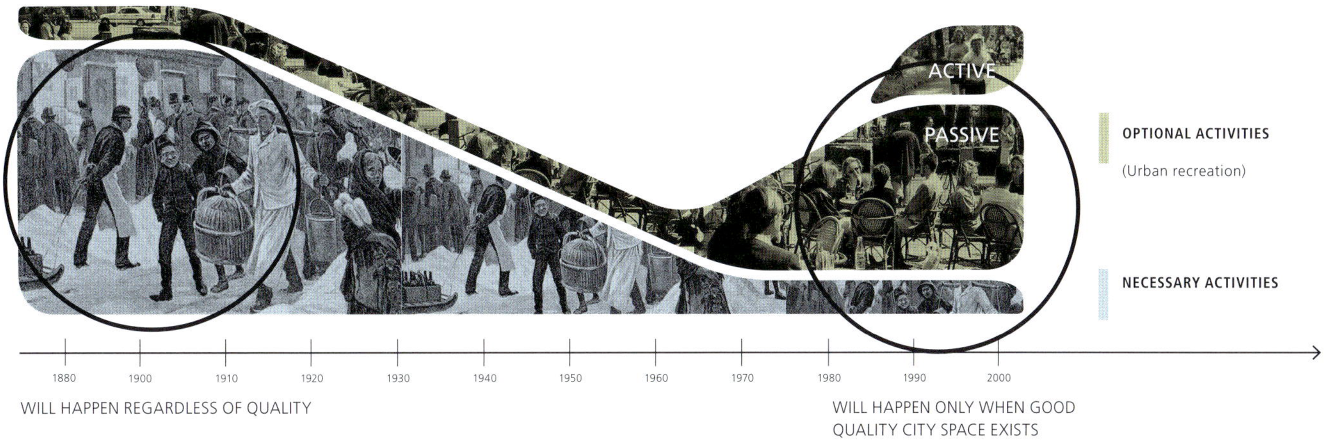

The Whale: Diagram showing the dramatic changes in the character of city life during the 20th century. Necessary activities dominate around 1900. The streets are crowded with people engaged in daily activities. Toward the end of the century, optional activities become much more prominent. While necessary activities go on regardless of the quality provided, the optional activities of the leisure-time society are dependent on good quality city spaces being provided.

Below: Nyhavn in Copenhagen on a summer day. All quality factors are nicely addressed and the space is crowded with people having a good time.

Protection

PROTECTION AGAINST TRAFFIC AND ACCIDENTS — FEELING SAFE

- Protection for pedestrians
- Eliminating fear of traffic

PROTECTION AGAINST CRIME AND VIOLENCE — FEELING SECURE

- Lively public realm
- Eyes on the street
- Overlapping functions day and night
- Good lighting

PROTECTION AGAINST UNPLEASANT SENSORY EXPERIENCES

- Wind
- Rain/snow
- Cold/heat
- Pollution
- Dust, noise, glare

Comfort

OPPORTUNITIES TO WALK

- Room for walking
- No obstacles
- Good surfaces
- Accessibility for everyone
- Interesting façades

OPPORTUNITIES TO STAND/STAY

- Edge effect/ attractive zones for standing/staying
- Supports for standing

OPPORTUNITIES TO SIT

- Zones for sitting
- Utilizing advantages: view, sun, people
- Good places to sit
- Benches for resting

OPPORTUNITIES TO SEE

- Reasonable viewing distances
- Unhindered sightlines
- Interesting views
- Lighting (when dark)

OPPORTUNITIES TO TALK AND LISTEN

- Low noise levels
- Street furniture that provides "talkscapes"

OPPORTUNITIES FOR PLAY AND EXERCISE

- Invitations for creativity, physical activity, exercise, and play
- By day and night
- In summer and winter

Delight

SCALE

- Buildings and spaces designed to human scale

OPPORTUNITIES TO ENJOY THE POSITIVE ASPECTS OF CLIMATE

- Sun/shade
- Heat/coolness
- Breeze

POSITIVE SENSORY EXPERIENCES

- Good design and detailing
- Good materials
- Fine views
- Trees, plants, water

Keyword list: 12 quality criteria concerning the pedestrian landscape

After years of research a list of 12 criteria important for the quality of the people landscapes has been developed. It is divided into 3 sections dealing with protection, comfort, and delight. After having been used as a teaching tool for many years in the School of Architecture in Copenhagen, it was first published in New City Life *to evaluate 28 streets and squares in the city center as well as in outlying districts of Copenhagen.*

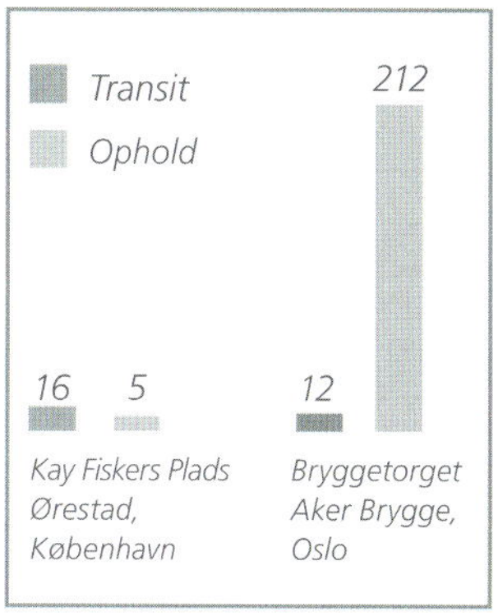

Comparing two modern squares, one in a new town in Copenhagen (top), the other in a new city district in Oslo, Norway (bottom). While the Norwegian square has addressed nearly all the 12 quality criteria, the Danish square has managed to disregard most of these concerns. Even with the same number of pedestrians passing through, the good-quality square has 10 times more people present.

The other part of the book describes a number of basic types of public spaces: promenades, central city spaces, ceremonial spaces, quiet spaces, waterfront spaces, empty spaces, and so on. As "quality for people" was now increasingly an important concern, the book goes on to introduce a keyword list of 12 quality criteria identified as important, which the authors used to evaluate and characterize 28 urban spaces throughout Copenhagen. This was the first time a city had conducted such an extensive overview of how their public spaces were used by their citizens over a full year.

CITIES FOR PEOPLE, 2010

Jan Gehl

Jan is often asked: "What is the difference between *Life Between Buildings* and *Cities for People?*" His answer is always brief: 40 years. *Cities for People* covers 40 years of Jan's research and years spent testing the ideas presented in *Life Between Buildings* in cities around the world. In *Cities for People* Jan revisits and reformulates the basic ideas, principles, and arguments that he originally presented in *Life Between Buildings* in 1971. It was his goal "to tell it all."

The Place Book Award for 2011 was one of several awards and favorable listings awarded to Cities for People.

The Realdania Foundation played an important role, not only in the funding, but in insisting that Jan write up "everything he knew" while he was still deeply involved with the theory and practice of life between buildings. As with most of his books, a very capable team of colleagues was behind the scenes. Foremost in the team were the two PhD graduates from the Center for Public Space Research, Camilla Richter-Friis van Deurs and Birgitte Bundesen Svarre. At this point, as Jan had retired from the School of Architecture in 2006, the various research projects, including this book, were anchored at Gehl Architects. The Danish version was published by Bogværket and the English version was published by Island Press.

As is the case with *Life Between Buildings* and with most of his other books, *Cities for People* primarily draws on Jan's studies, experience, and examples from his own career, with "not many detours made to what others may have thought or found over the years." It is a book about the themes as seen through Jan's eyes. It is a very personal statement, and what he sees as his main contribution to this field.

True to the established Jan Gehl tradition, this book was also carefully composed with the graphics and photos visually retelling the

The change in paradigms for city planning is a primary subject for discussion in Cities for People. *After many years of modernist city planning and automobile invasion, good cities for the twenty-first century are expected to be lively, livable, safe, sustainable, and healthy.*

stories in the rather simple, straightforward text. *Cities for People* conveys Jan's messages in a way easily understood by many different groups of readers in many different cultures.

The book begins by discussing the two dominating paradigms for planning in the second half of the twenty-first century: modernism and the invasion of the motorcar. In this context, the human dimension was completely overlooked and discarded. Nothing really was known about how drastically these new planning principles influenced people's use of public spaces.

By 2010, it was possible to show, through examples, how strongly invitations could influence behavior in cities. Inviting cars leads to more traffic. Inviting pedestrians, public life, and bicycling leads to impressive changes in the ways people used public spaces. This is illustrated through the examples of Copenhagen, Melbourne, New York, and many other places. Throughout, Jan highlights the role of the city as meeting place in present day society.

The second chapter goes into great detail describing the importance of human senses and the handling of scale in cities as a key factor in well-being and the use of city spaces. This idea is a key part of the book. The human scale had been almost completely forgotten

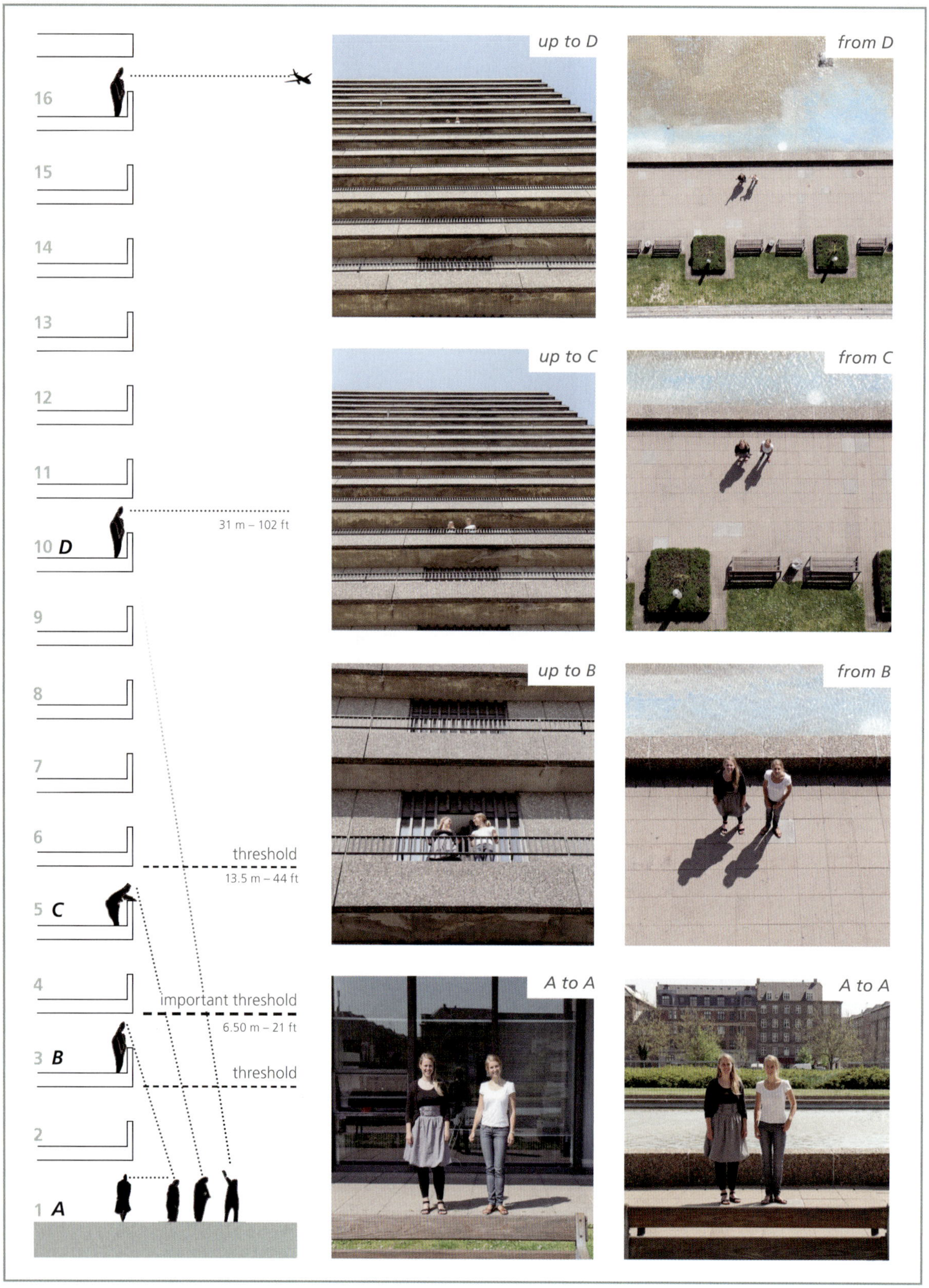

16
15
14
13
12
11
10 D
31 m – 102 ft
9
8
7
6
threshold
13.5 m – 44 ft
5 C
4
important threshold
6.50 m – 21 ft
3 B
threshold
2
1 A
up to D
from D
up to C
from C
up to B
from B
A to A
A to A

In Cities for People, *as previously in* Life Between Buildings, *great emphasis is placed on discussing the biological history of man, how the human senses have developed, and how they work in relation to architecture and city spaces. Understanding the human body, human senses, and human behavior is an important key for creating cities for people. Shown at left is a study of human senses in relation to a highrise building. At right is a study on the importance of closeness and small dimensions.*

in the era of modernist planners and traffic engineers. Jan sees "a rekindling of careful work with scale" as one of the most important challenges for creating cities for people.

The book then introduces the new, emerging planning paradigm: *wanted for the 21st century are cities which are lively, safe, sustainable, and healthy.* Each of the four aspects is investigated in more detail. For each aspect, examples are presented, explaining how life between buildings can be invited and stimulated in the present-day society situation. The developing concerns for personal safety are discussed as well as various ways of addressing these concerns. Jan points out that the solutions that work for people-oriented planning are also solutions that very effectively create more sustainable and healthy cities. He emphasizes that "more walking and bicycling is, in a very direct way, good for the climate and good for the health of each individual participant. Indeed, the general and eternal arguments for caring for people in cities are strongly supported by these emerging concerns for sustainable cities and healthy lifestyles."

Later chapters show, in more detail, how to go about creating cities for people. As in *Life Between Buildings,* Jan argues that the quality of the city at eye-level is crucial for success, and in great detail he describes the good city for walking, standing, sitting, seeing, hearing, playing, bicycling, and so on.

Under the heading "Life, Space and Buildings—And in This Order, Please" are presented principles for making new city plans and neighborhoods. Jan describes how the modernists invariably used the order: building, space, and then perhaps life. But life in the public spaces never thrived with this prioritization. Using the opposite order follows the way older cities were developed, and Jan challenges that this is also the way to go with contemporary, people-oriented urban design. Life first, then space, then buildings. New, in relation to Jan's books, is a short chap-

Left: Contact between building and street is possible from the lowest five floors. Contact with the city quickly dissipates above the fifth floor, with the contact interface changing to views, clouds, and airplanes.

ter on the planning challenges posed by the fast-growing cities in the developing world. Selected examples from Curitiba, Bogotá, and Cape Town are presented, showing the need for safe, lively public space in all parts of the world. This chapter points out that by far the greatest challenges in creating cities for people are to be found in the developing world, as well as the greatest need for safe, healthy public space. At the very least good public space and good conditions for walking, bicycling, and public transport should be created. Infrastructure for people is the cheapest and most easily implemented infrastructure of all.

A toolbox is included in the final pages of the book with the major tools, checklists, and key diagrams published in the various earlier books presented. The toolbox sums up key elements from the many years of research.

The book was given a flying start by being published simultaneously in Copenhagen, Washington, DC and Beijing. The message was no longer primarily for the benefit of the Danes. In the four decades since the publication of *Life Between Buildings,* these issues had increasingly become of global concern.

The reaction to *Cities for People* has been equally widespread, with placements in a number of lists of influential books on planning and sustainable cities, including the 2011 *Great Places Book Award* issued by EDRA (Environmental Design Research Association and the PLACES Magazine).

Even in view of the flying start with versions in Danish, English, and Chinese, the printing history of *Cities for People* has been remarkable. By 2016, the book had been published or contracted for publishing in more than 30 languages including Marathi (India), Farsi (Iran), Albanian, Georgian, Kazakh, and Estonian. Also, a novelty for Jan's books, this book has become available in Arabic, German, and even in French (as a result of "devoted efforts by the good people of Quebec").

The launch of the Czech edition of Cities for People *in Prague in 2012 was a grand affair involving the Danish Ambassador Ole E. Jensby and the official embassy cargo bike, complete with shield and Danish flag.*

Above: The team behind Cities for People *photographed outside the Danish Architecture Centre at the launch in 2010. From left: Karen Steenhard, Rikke Sode, Birgitte Svarre, Isabell Duckett, Jan Gehl, Mariken L. Helle, Camilla Richter-Friis van Deurs, Andrea Have, and Lars Gemzøe.*

Below: By 2016, Cities for People *has been published (or contracted for publishing) in 24 languages. A further 8 versions are in various stages of preparation. Above all, this points to a strong, and rapidly growing interest in creating more people-friendly cities.*

Printing history as of 2016

HOW TO STUDY PUBLIC LIFE, 2013

Jan Gehl & Birgitte Svarre

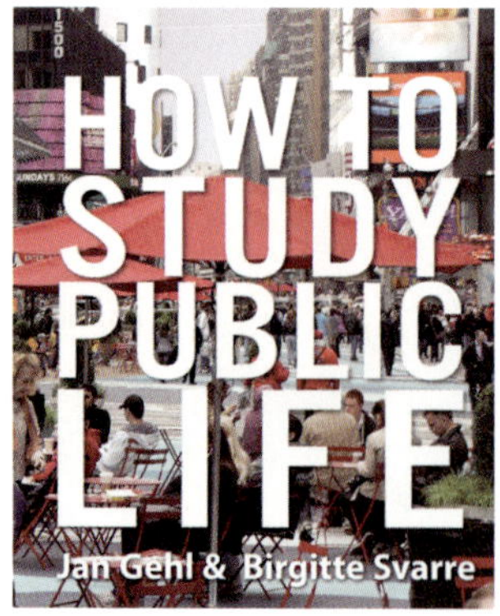

The book How to Study Public Life *aims to give an overview of the study methods developed over many years of research. Right: Some of the basic tools developed for carrying out observation studies.*

This sixth book is different from the other five. It is not about life in public spaces or about the physical environment, but still touches both subjects in explaining ways in which public life can be studied, recorded, and systematized.

As was the case with *Cities for People,* this book was also inspired (and funded) by the Realdania Foundation, which suggested that the study methods developed in Denmark since the 1960s ought to be described for others to use. Jan was told, again very politely, that "this ought to be done while he could still remember the finer details." Given the fact that the continuation of the research tradition was now at Gehl Architects, the new book on methods was developed in this framework. Birgitte Svarre became co-author and the anchor person on the project.

The book describes how the studies of the interaction between public life and built form in public spaces have attained the distinct contours of a professional field, with its own tools, practitioners, directions, and "schools." The book is, however, quite faithful to the Copenhagen practice of emphasizing observation tools. General research questions for public life studies such as Who?, What?, Where?, When?, How fast?, How long? and How many? are presented, and various methods to understand these questions are discussed. The development of this fledgling professional field is described, including profiles of the (mostly American) pioneers. A major part of the book, both in volume and information, is an extensive chapter called "How They Did It: Research Notes" in which 20 research stories are presented. This part is a foray into the streets, squares, and parks in many corners of the world and brings the readers very close to the many daily scenes studied. The majority of cases come from studies made by the Copenhagen team, and true to the traditions of this particular "school," the methods displayed are closely related to the architectural background of the team members. Their training in measuring, recording, and documenting is clearly seen. Since the aim of this book is to provide a wider overview of what has been happening internationally in this field and the other approaches that have been developed, this chapter also presents a number of case studies based on other research cultures.

The two final chapters of the book describe how this multitude of methods, and the new insights brought to architecture and planning by way of these tools, has been applied to real-life projects, foremost in cities and mostly in the form of Public Space Public Life studies directly based on the methods developed

Basic tools for observation studies

Counting

Counting is a widely used tool in public life studies. In principle, everything can be counted, providing numbers for making before-and-after comparisons, between different geographic areas over time.

Looking for traces

Human activity often leaves traces, which can give the observer information about city life. Traces can be counted, photographed, or drawn on a map.

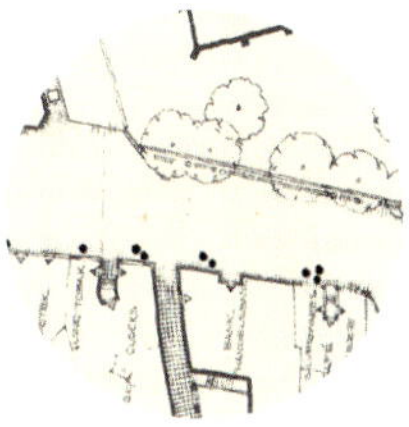

Plotting

Activities, people, places for staying, and much more can be plotted (i.e., drawn as symbols on a plan of an area being studied) to mark the number and type of activities and where they take place. This is also called behavioral mapping.

Photographing

Photographing is an essential part of public life studies as it helps to document whether urban life and form interact or don't after changes have been made.

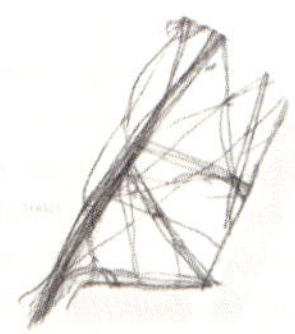

Tracing

People's movements inside or crossing limited spaces can be drawn as lines of movement on the plan of the study area.

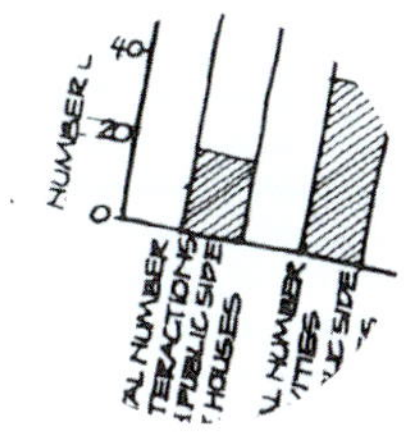

Keeping a diary

Keeping a diary can register details and nuances about the interaction between public life and space. Noting observations can later be categorized and/or quantified.

Tracking

In order to observe people's movements over a large area or for a longer time, observers can discreetly follow people without their knowing it or follow someone who knows and agrees to be followed and observed. This is also called shadowing.

Test walks

Taking a walk while observing can be made more or less systematic, so that the observer sees problems and potentials for himself on any given route.

Case study: Conditions for walking in the city center of Sydney

A frequently used tool for assessing the conditions for walking in a city is the test walk. Walking between various destinations is evaluated and timed in order to document how many obstacles and how much wait time is encountered on the selected routes. The example on this page is from a test walk in Sydney. It shows very long wait times, especially when walking on the east-west routes.

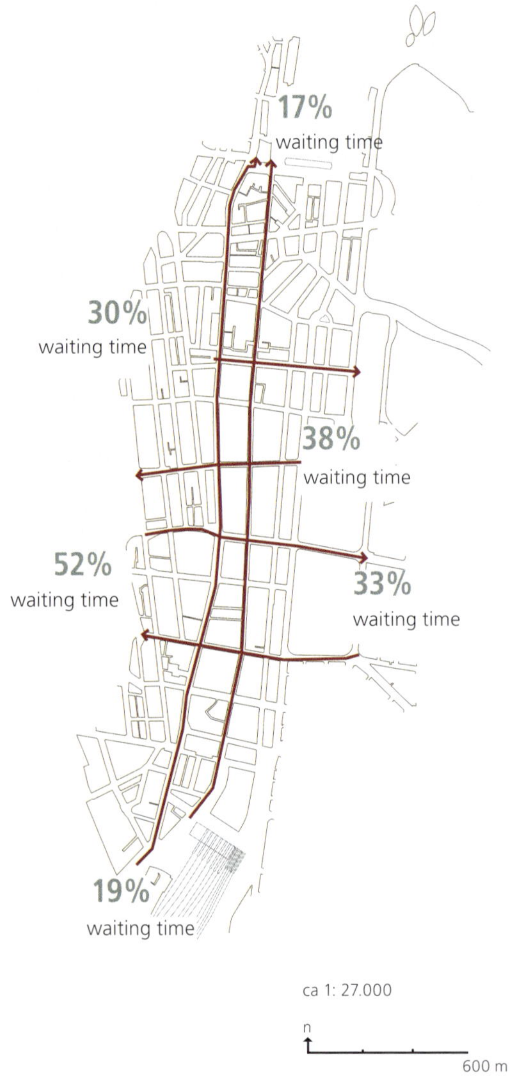

for the City of Copenhagen. How this type of study is now being used in cities of all sizes around the world, from small provincial cities to major international cities like London, New York, and Moscow is shown. Gradually, through the systematic studies of how people use the cities, new ways of thinking and new people-oriented ways of planning public space are enabled.

The final chapter goes on to present how Public Space Public Life studies can be a political factor that, over time, can change the mindsets and lead to dramatic improvements for the users of a city, as shown dramatically through the Copenhagen example.

How to Study Public Life is one of the first handbooks explaining how to document how people use their cities, and has achieved widespread interest. Since it was published in 2013 in Danish by Bogvaerket and in English by Island Press, Korean, German, Romanian, Japanese, Iranian, Russian, and Chinese editions have been or are about to be published.

While the popularity of the other books would suggest a growing support for the ideas among the general public, the popularity of *How to Study Public Life* would suggest that this new professional field is steadily gaining momentum.

Printing History by 2016

Danish

English

Korean

Romanian

Chinese

Japanese

German

Bourke St

6

CHANGING CITIES

CHANGING CITIES

"Cities—like books—can be read, and Jan Gehl understands their language."
—Lord Richard Rogers, Architect, Chief Advisor on Architecture and Urbanism to Mayor of London Ken Livingston (2000–2008)

The move to assisting cities started around 1990 as a "kitchen-table" operation and a "distinct sideshow" to Jan's work with the urban design department at the School of Architecture. The neighboring countries saw how Copenhagen was benefitting from the detailed studies on how its public space was functioning. Inspired first to invite Jan to undertake similar studies was Oslo (1988), followed quickly by Stockholm (1990). The Oslo study was carried out as an academic study with much data collection, as the Copenhagen ones had been to this point, leaving the Norwegians to draw their own conclusions. Finding this academic model too restricting, the Stockholm study became the first Public Space Public Life survey completed by Jan as a private consultant. In this way, he extended the study to cover both "Space" and "Life" surveys and provided "Recommendations" outlining what to do to improve the city center. Stockholm was an especially interesting city to study and to advise. Having survived two world wars without much damage, the city leaders in Stockholm in the 1940s and 1950s decided to tear down their inner city in order to rebuild it as a state-of-the-art modernist city center. Ironically, in the end, it came to look very much like the rebuilt war-torn cities of Germany and England, and also came to look and function quite a bit like Melbourne and Perth in Australia. The Stockholm study came to have quite an influence on the future development of the city. Looking back, Jan explains how it was personal academic connections in these two cities that led to the Copenhagen studies spreading north.

Academic connections were also behind Jan's first contacts with Australia and with his first Public Space Public Life study outside Scandinavia, the Perth Study of 1993–1994. Following the Perth study was the first study in Melbourne in 1994, leading over the next twenty or so years to studies in nearly all major Australian and New Zealand cities, making it fair to say that "it all started down under."

In addition to the first down-under studies, further kitchen-table studies were being undertaken during this time in various Danish provincial cities, foremost Odense. Jan undertook an interesting task in 1998 for the City of Edinburgh—one of the world's most beautiful cities and a UNESCO heritage site. The extraordinary qualities of the city had, however, not saved the city from an unusually crude treatment from the traffic planners. Jan's 1998 report was, while rather brief, very critical, urging a serious upgrade of the public realm in this unique city.

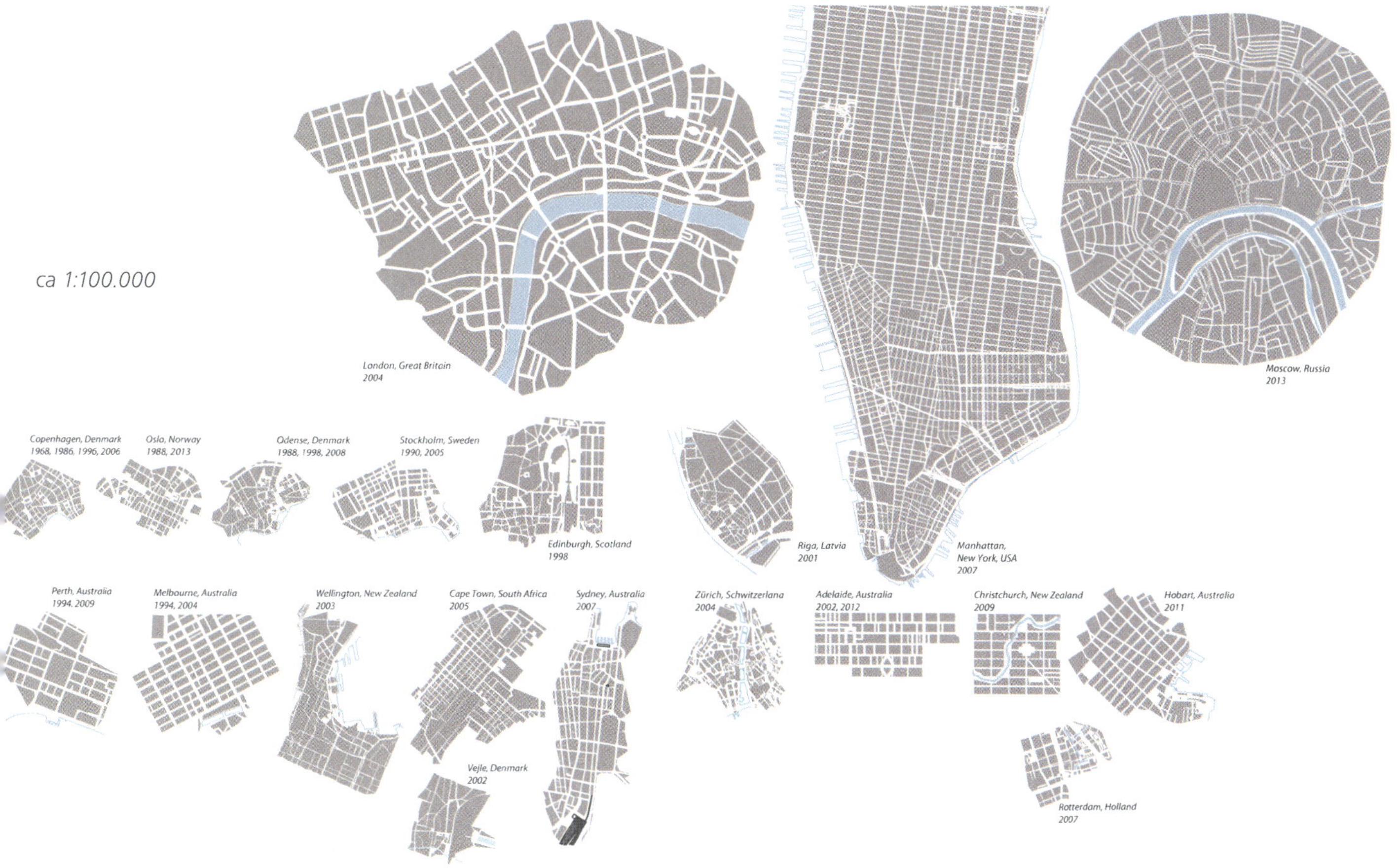

Overview of the cities where Jan has been directly involved in conducting Public Space Public Life surveys. The plans show the study areas in the respective cities, except in the case of London, New York, and Moscow where only selected streets, squares, and parks in the central city districts shown on the plans have been studied.

As more clients knocked on Jan's door, the kitchen-table office, staffed with an ever-changing collection of former urban design students, Jan (and especially Ingrid) realized that the time had come to set out in a more professional manner. In 2000, when Jan was 63 years old, he founded Gehl Architects—urban quality consultants, with architect Helle Søholt as co-founder and CEO.

"Going professional" as consultants with Gehl Architects meant a big increase in the number of projects undertaken. Instead of dealing with potential clients defensively, Jan would say, "I would love to come to your city, but only after the exams." It was now possible for Jan to be positive and quick when attending to the growing number of requests—"If you want liveable, sustainable, and healthy cities we can help you—soon."

Along with the Australian and New Zealand cities, work in a number of European cities (Drammen, Norway, 2002; Riga, Latvia, 2001; Zürich, Switzerland, 2004; Rotterdam, The Netherlands, 2007) and some smaller towns in Scandinavia was carried out in the first decade of the twenty-first century. And in 2003-2004 "the big league was joined," meaning Jan worked for the first time on a major "big" city, London. Over a number of years, Jan's lectures and work for the Public Realm Advisory Group (PRAG)—chaired by architect Richard Rogers, Mayor Ken Livingstone's chief advisor on architecture and urbanism—led to a number of contacts, which in turn, led to Gehl Architects being invited to conduct its first Public Space Public Life study in a major city. The study, described in more detail later in the chapter, came to have a direct bearing on Gehl Architects being commissioned to work for New York starting in 2007. Once again, Jan had, through a series of lectures in New York, raised the awareness about the need for an inviting city and established a number of valuable contacts, especially Janette Sadik-Khan. When Mayor Michael Bloomberg, in 2007, announced his famous PlaNYC to make New York much more sustainable, the direct link to Copenhagen had already been made. Shortly after, Janette Sadik-Khan became the commissioner of the New York Department of Transportation. She and commissioner of planning Amanda Burden came to Copenhagen to see the city for themselves, and from this point the involvement of Jan and Gehl Architects unfolded in New York.

In one of his now standard lectures at the Eco-Cities conference in Montreal in 2011, Jan told "tall tales" about how Copenhagen, Melbourne, Sydney, London, and New York were all well on their way to be more liveable and sustainable, all spurred on by Public Space Public Life surveys. After the lecture, Minister Anton Kulbashevsky, Deputy Mayor of Moscow came forward and immediately invited Jan and Gehl Architects to come to Moscow and lend a caring hand to improving his city. Before the end of 2011, Jan and team started working in Moscow. By 2013, the study was presented, and by 2016, remarkable results were visible all over this huge city.

Since the Moscow study, quite a number of other studies have followed in big and small cities on several continents. The work is still unfolding in many directions with various teams from Gehl Architects expanding the work and cities around the world undertaking their versions of the surveys. After the Moscow study, the next generation at Gehl Architects, under the direction of partner and director Henriette Vamberg, carried on the work.

Jan was directly involved in the city projects described in this chapter and led as project manager, usually with Henriette Vamberg as "team and soul mate." These cities were chosen because they are all places that Jan feels are "his" cities. He is "much attached to each and every one of these persons and places."

The cities included in this chapter demonstrate Jan's impact on cities. However the cities themselves have progressed from Jan's surveys and the discoveries he made, his work and thinking has had a lasting legacy.

JAN GEHL AND THE CITIES OF AUSTRALIA AND NEW ZEALAND

Work with the various Australian cities started in 1993 and is still in progress. Several cities have had follow-up surveys. All major cities in Australia and New Zealand (except Canberra) have utilized the advice from Jan and his teams over the years.

Starting with guest professorships in Melbourne and Perth in the 1970s, Jan has a long history with Australia and a special affinity for the place and the culture, particularly the sense of humor, the informality, and the widespread interest in livable and sustainable cities. Along with Perth (1993–1994 and 2008–2009), and Melbourne (1994 and 2004), Jan and Gehl Architects' influence and commitments in Australia spread mainly through word of mouth, resulting in commisions for many other Australian cities, including Adelaide, which also has had two Public Space Public Life surveys (2002 and 2011), Sydney (2007; where work is still progressing), Brisbane (a suburban study commissioned by the Queensland Government, 2009), Hobart (2010), Launceston (2010), and Wollongong (2014). Jan has also been busy in New Zealand. He and his teams have worked for the cities of Wellington (2004), Christchurch (2009 and again after the big earthquake in 2011), as well as Auckland (2009–2010).

Said in other words, the ideas "have spread like a bushfire down under." In no part of the world has Jan's tale on the importance of doing people-oriented city planning caught on more extensively than in Australia and New Zealand, where by now, every major city in both countries (with Canberra as the only exception from the rule) is using planning principles originating from Scandinavia as guidelines for their development. Jan has always insisted that the general outlook on quality of life and quality of cities in Scandinavia and Australasia have many similarities. Looking at the lists of livable cities of the world, it is evident that cities from these two regions occupy the majority of the top places in most of the lists, reflecting that quality issues in city planning have a high priority in both regions.

GEHL ARCHITECTS –THE JAN GEHL STORY

Helle Søholt and Jan Gehl.

On May 1, 2000, Jan partnered with Helle Søholt to establish Gehl Architects. Helle Søholt graduated as an architect in 1998 from the urban design department at the School of Architecture in Copenhagen. Following her Copenhagen studies, Helle moved to the University of Washington in Seattle to obtain a master's degree in urban design. On and off during this period, Helle also helped Jan in his kitchen-table office, and thus became an obvious partner for the new planning firm. From the very start, it was established that Helle would look after the running of the firm while Jan's role would be to provide insights from his years of research.

The new company quickly gained momentum, working in Copenhagen and a number of other cities, mostly in Australia, as well as on new town projects in Ireland and Norway. In just five years, the number of clients and projects had grown dramatically; so had the number of employees. Even with the economic recession between 2008 and 2011, the company saw a steady growth in the number of projects and in the number of countries where projects were conducted. The challenge of diverse projects was met by employing people with many different profiles. All this and more can be read on www.gehlpeople.com.

Over the years, Helle has proven her talent for leadership, enabling Gehl Architects to grow in quality and size, establishing branch offices in New York and San Francisco, and by 2016, running a staff of more than 70 (and still conducting the odd Public Space Public Life surveys for cities such as Almata, Kazakhstan; Shanghai, China; and Tokyo, Japan, but by now also undertaking many more and different types of projects).

In 2011, when Jan was 75, he started to back out of the company, withdrawing as partner and selling his part of the company to the next generation. By 2016, Gehl Architects had six new partners, and Jan, as a rather independent senior advisor, can enjoy seeing the next generation continue to carry his ideas to the far corners of the world.

Gehl Architects, 2008

MELBOURNE, AUSTRALIA 1994–2004

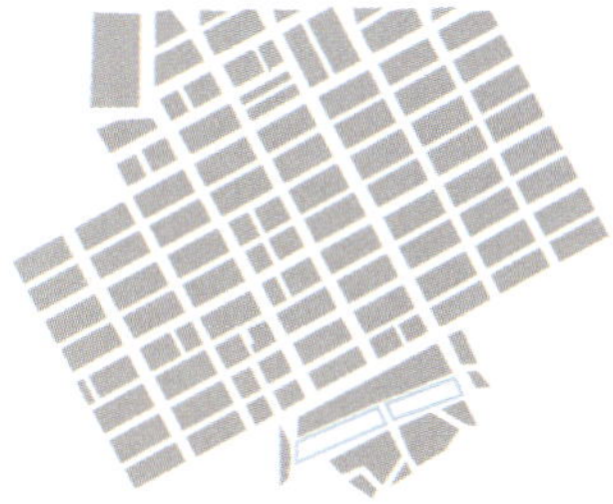

Melbourne study area ca 1:50.000

Melbourne, Australia is now consistently named one of the world's most liveable cities.[46] But it has not always been that way. The City of Melbourne has achieved this coveted status through incremental, coordinated, and consistent changes toward a more people-focused city.

The changes that have happened within the City of Melbourne, championed by Rob Adams as Director of Design, are among those that Jan considers to be most impressive. Jan was invited by the City to collaborate on two Public Space Public Life surveys—the first in 1994 and the second in 2004 (with Gehl Architects and Jan as team leader). The two surveys show a dramatic change toward Melbourne being a much more people-focused city and helping considerably in becoming the 'most liveable city in the world' based on the the Economist Intelligence Unit ranking for 2014 and 2015.

When Jan was a visiting professor at the University of Melbourne and the Royal Melbourne Institute of Technology in the 1970s, Melbourne's city center was in decline both economically and in terms of population. Studies from the Victorian State Government

Gehl Architects and the City of Melbourne were awarded the 2006 Australian Urban Design Award for their contribution to improving the quality of city life in Australia.

Melbourne was always a city of streets. Squares, however, are very important for developing a multifaceted public life. Today, Melbourne has not one but two very fine urban spaces: City Hall Square and Federation Square (shown at left), which is rated as the best public square in Australia.

The transformation of Melbourne has involved a general widening of the sidewalks, paving with bluestones, numerous street trees, and one of the best street furnishing programs in the world. Shown above and left is Swanston Street before and after refurbishment.

and the NGO Committee for Melbourne (established in 1985) set up the agenda for reinvigorating the city center into a "lively, attractive hub for the more than three million inhabitants in the region."[47] But the street-level detail was missing.

When Rob Adams invited Jan to assist the city in undertaking a Public Space Public Life survey of the city center in 1994, he wanted a professional dialogue concerning where the city was in terms of achieving a lively and attractive city center and public realm. Working closely with Adams, Jan surveyed the city, and together they developed a list of necessary and ambitious goals focused on urban improvements.

Over the next ten years, the City of Melbourne and the state government implemented a comprehensive program that included improvements to streets and laneways, the creation of new squares, far more residences in the city center; a reduction in road capacity, enhancements to the famous Melbourne tramways, and programs to encourage new commercial activity.

The result has been a dramatic turnaround in the central city economy with all major economic, population, and tourist indicators showing impressive improvements. Underlying these have been the improvements related to the public space public life work by Jan and, not least, the strong leadership of Rob Adams.

Jan describes it this way: the city was "transformed from a city where people once rushed to the office and back home again . . . like ants to their various places and when they are finished they go down like ants in the hole again" to "a city which really is very inviting for promenading, and for lingering, sitting, and enjoying."[48] In his talks, Jan frequently claims that "Melbourne, by now, has an atmosphere and quality almost like Paris, but the weather is much better."

Reinvigorating the many small service lanes stands out as one of the most remarkable accomplishments in Melbourne.

The ambitious bicycle infrastructure program is using Copenhagen-style bicycle lanes. Parked cars are used to protect the bicyclists, rather than using the bicyclists to protect the parked cars as is still seen in many cities.

According to Rob Adams, one reason for the success of the Melbourne Public Space Public Life survey, titled "Places for People," was that the recommendations and goals of the surveys were undertaken as a collaboration between Jan, Gehl Architects, and the city council, and then approved by the city council and integrated with their projects and strategic work.[49] The surveys and the transition to making the city people-focused were ongoing, and consistently implemented over many years, demonstrating the clear and constant commitment of the city. The Public Space Public Life surveys helped to gain support for implementation of the program.

The City of Melbourne now routinely counts the number of pedestrians, using electronic counters placed at important locations throughout the city. In addition, they have been undertaking their own surveys of public life and, in 2015, the City released a walking plan based on an economic assessment of value of walking to the city. Systematic documentation and consideration of public space and public life are now routine for the city. Jan considers this the way all cities should work with public life.

MY JAN GEHL STORY

by Robert Adams, Director, City Design and Projects, City of Melbourne

Having assisted with the writing of the 1985 Strategy Plan for the City, I had been asked to stay on and implement the plan. In essence, the plan's vision was that the City, which was in steady decline through the 1980s, should attempt to become a "24-hour city that looked and felt like Melbourne." With little revenue, the strategy was one of incremental development, building on Melbourne's existing strengths.

I first met Jan in 1993. After nearly ten years of implementation across a broad spectrum of projects in Melbourne, it had become apparent that because of the very nature of these projects, namely small scale and incremental, the community would, like slowly warming up in a bath, not notice the changes taking place. With this in mind, and aware of the work that Jan had been doing in measuring the changes in cities, we decided to make contact and see if he would advise us on how best to measure and tell our story.

The result was the first *Places for People* publication in 1994 for which our teams collaborated in measuring the elements of city life and amenity. While the first set of data was important as a benchmark, what we had not anticipated was the impact that Jan's knowledge and enthusiasm would bring to our cause. He was, in his renowned manner, instantly able to champion and promote the many changes and challenges we were tackling. As an outside voice, he cut through the normal reluctance to believe the local voices, and he helped us to sell the agenda for the next ten years. He also became a close and valued friend with whom I could compare ideas and share knowledge.

Over the following ten years, Jan would visit Melbourne on a number of occasions to attend conferences and speaking engagements at which he would promote the cause of good urban design. Impressed with our approach and willingness to measure progress, he started an international campaign to promote what Melbourne was doing, a campaign that has seen Melbourne featured widely on the international stage.

A major step forward for Melbourne had been made in 1992, just prior to the first study with Jan. The City had put in place an ambitious program to reintroduce residential to the central city. The program, called Postcode 3000, built on the property market crash of the late 1980s to use vacant commercial office space and convert it to residential. The 1985 plan had called for 15,000 new residential units in the city center over the next 15 years. The program was highly successful and saw the number of the residential apartments grow from 685 in 1985 to 15,000 by the year 2000. Off the back of this success, and the continued expanded program of incremental changes, the city had completely changed by the time our second collaboration with Jan occurred in 2004.

The second study, "Places for People 2004" was a more sophisticated version of the 1994 study and clearly illustrated the significant transformation that had taken place in central Melbourne over the previous 20 years. It also made recommendations that built on the continuity already in place. The refined presentation and accessibility to data that the Gehl collaboration had brought about enabled this story of transformation to be clearly told. Jan's advocacy and communication of the Melbourne story became more international and worked alongside the increased international events and the Commonwealth Games of 2006 to promote Melbourne onto the international stage.

My personal friendship and admiration of Jan's knowledge and enthusiasm had grown through the years and was further enhanced by a six-month sabbatical in Copenhagen in the latter part of 2006.

During this time, I was fortunate enough to share Jan's dual working experience through the Center for Public Space Research he set up at the School of Architecture and also at his office alongside Helle, Lars, and the talented Gehl team, which was a real privilege. Their values and collaborative approach gave a real insight into why they have become such a formidable force in the urban design field. Outside the university, we worked on a study for the German Federal Ministry of Transport, Building, and Urban Affairs in preparation for Germany taking over the chairmanship of the EU. The study "Baukultur - as an impulse for growth, good examples for European cities," looked at 12 case studies of how cities had managed to turn their fortunes around. Melbourne, although not a European example, managed to find its way in. Since this time, our friendship has endured the tyranny of distance and we have worked together on a number of city projects, including New York, where our shared lessons have helped contribute.

My greatest joy has been to see the recognition that Jan has belatedly received for his formative thinking, starting with *Life Between Buildings,* which in my mind sits alongside *The Death and Life of Great American Cities* by Jane Jacobs as one of the most important urban design texts of the 20th century. His influence on the importance of cities as the economic, social, and environmental drivers of our world economy is only now being realized, and as he approaches 80, he shows no sign of slowing down.

Moving to Melbourne might not be a bad idea. The city has repeatedly been named as one of the most livable cities in the world.

LONDON, UNITED KINGDOM 2002–2004

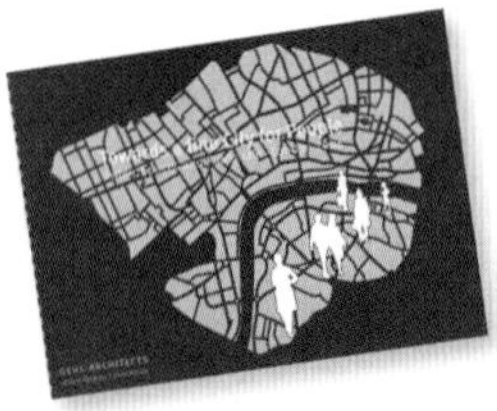

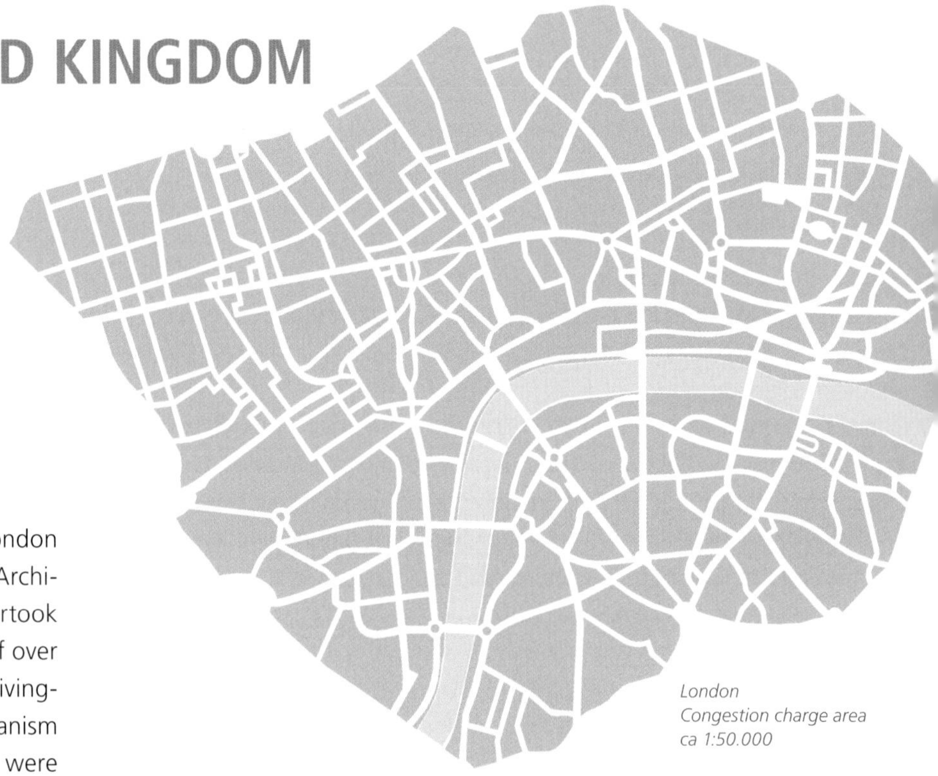

London
Congestion charge area
ca 1:50.000

The Public Space Public Life study in London was a milestone for Jan and Gehl Architects. It marks the first time he undertook surveys in a major metropolis—a city of over 7 million people. London Mayor Ken Livingstone, along with his advisor on urbanism and architecture, Lord Richard Rogers, were dedicated to "bringing people back into the city, and emphasizing the importance of high-quality design."[50] In 2003, the city enacted a congestion charge for vehicles entering the city center in a rather large area, compromising some 23 square kilometers in the center of London.

The London Public Space Public Life study was commissioned by Transport for London and Central London Partnership and undertaken in 2003–2004.[51] Due to its scale and complexity (in addition to the size of the city center, many functional centers have emerged far from it), the study required the development of new survey tools and methods. It required careful consideration of location as it was not possible to study the whole city center but only selected areas and aspects. The Acupuncture Approach had to be introduced. This approach used surveys of selected streets, squares, and parks chosen as representative samples, which when seen together showed typical aspects of the problems and potentials to be found in the big and complex city.

What the survey found was that London had many attractive qualities, but it was overwhelmed with traffic and was particularly difficult for people with mobility limitations, like the elderly, disabled, or people in wheelchairs or pushing strollers. The findings showed a city in which sidewalks were inadequate to accommodate the numbers of pedestrians in many places. The sidewalks were overcrowded and numerous obstacles forced pedestrians to find their own routes. Crossing streets was generally very complicated. People needed to push buttons and politely apply to cross. Then they had to run fast to get across before the blinking light turned red. Signage was inadequate and confusing, and public spaces generally lacked seating. Pedestrian movement patterns and the number of

> *"The intention of the report is to act as a catalyst for change demonstrating to key decision makers and delivery agents how London's public space could be transformed."*[52]
>
> Patricia Brown, Chief Executive at Central London Partnership

London may have many merits, but the quality of the pedestrian landscape seen by the Gehl Architect team in 2003 was just short of appalling.

A simple set of questions were used for assessing the quality of the pedestrian environment: Walking along? Getting across? Getting around? Sitting? Hearing and talking? Climate at eye level? Aesthetics and design? The situation after dark?

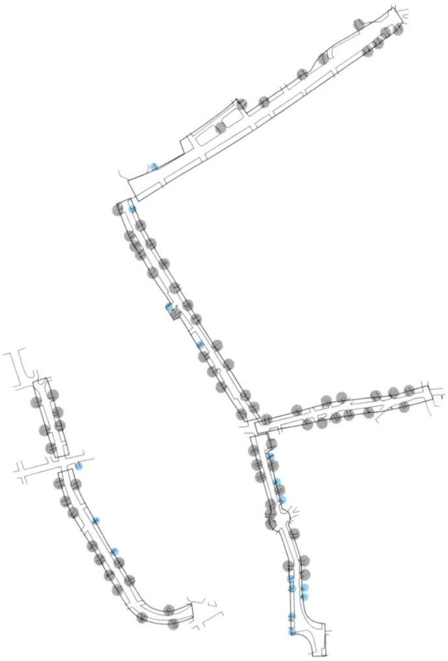

Unnecessary sidewalk interruptions were found to be a London speciality. In the streets studied, including Regent Street and Tottenham Court Road, a total of 74 unnecessary sidewalk interruptions were found, as shown on the inserted street plan

people walking were largely undocumented before Jan and the team from Gehl Architects were brought in.

In the report of his findings called "Toward a Fine City for People", Jan and Gehl Architects recommended a strategy of incremental changes, focused primarily on changing perceptions of what London could be. The recommendations were focused on celebrating and capitalizing on London's unique qualities, including the numerous city squares and the riverfront of the Thames. A number of solutions were proposed, including: focusing on road safety, developing a coherent policy for pedestrians and an urban design policy, introducing pedestrian priority streets, using art, landscaping and seating, and making cycling easier through the city.

The influence in London was perceived to be more about changing mindsets than on-the-ground physical changes, although there have been a number of physical changes implemented subsequently. The changes that have occurred in London based at least partly on the work of Jan and Gehl Architects include more elements focused on recreation throughout the city, including a beach along the river; shared streets (such as Exhibition Road); the pedestrianization of Trafalgar Square; the redesign of Piccadilly Circus, and the addition of walkways along the South Bank.

Given the many public space quality shortcomings found in London in the 2004 study and the extensive recommendations presented in the report "Toward a Fine City for People," Jan has frequently aired his disappointment regarding the relative "slow pace of improvements" undertaken compared to cities like New York and Moscow. Both the political structure of the city, with many self-governing boroughs, and the stakeholder status where huge parts of London are owned by very few landowners can explain the difficult decision-making process. This could also explain why Gehl Architects has not been invited to conduct follow-up work with either the City or individual boroughs. However, a number of consultancies have been conducted for various big London estates after 2004, such as the extensive plans for upgrading selected streets and squares in Mayfair and Belgravia owned by the Grosvenor Estate.

Recent years have seen a number of improvements to the streets and squares in London. One new feature is the introduction of Summer Streets where a number of streets are closed to traffic on selected summer days. Shown here is a peaceful, car-free Regent street.

A system in which a few stakeholders own big parts of the city is why selected improvements are carried out by stakeholders rather than the various boroughs. Shown right is Mount Street in Mayfair before and after renovation. This project was part of a general strategy for upgrading Mayfair initiated by the Grosvenor Estate and planned by Gehl Architects.

AMMAN, JORDAN 2004–2006

The survey and work in Amman, Jordan, holds a special significance for Jan.

The work for the City of Amman started out in the same way as so many other city projects. Locally, interest in improving the city was developing, and through various channels, Jan was invited to come to Amman to lecture.

This lecture led to a collaboration between Jan, with a team from Gehl Architects, and the Amman Committee, a group of distinguished architects and academics entrusted by the king of Jordan to improve the capital city.

Jan and the team undertook a number of limited public life surveys and made suggestions for improving many areas and public spaces in Amman. One suggestion was to establish a completely new square in the Ashrafieh District in East Amman. This densely populated district, home to a very high number of refugees from Palestine, had virtually no open spaces. The idea was to create a large public square that reflected the diversity of the area, which contained an important mosque and the major hospital in the city. The resulting square came to provide a much-wanted recreational place in an area that was suffering from a lack of open space.

Other projects conducted for the Amman Committee included transforming Wakala

The City of Amman is in a spectacular setting, on a series of hills with the major roads in the valleys. Not only are the individual houses quite prominent in most views, but the roofs play an important part in the overall townscape. Rules for coloring the buildings and organizing the roof spaces secure a valuable visual identity.

Public open space was missing in the Ashrafieh district in East Amman. After identifying a potential site, a new square was established in 2007 (Abu Drweesh Mosque Square, urban design guidelines: Gehl Architects, project architect: Tibah Consultants/Ayamn Zuayter). Left: A view to the city has been established from the new square. Next page: Before and after the intervention.

Street in the Sweifieh District into a pedestrian-friendly street, improving the historic area around the old Roman theater, and planning for the relocation of proposed highrise buildings from the hill tops to selected valleys in order to protect the unique skyline of the city.

Looking back on the many cities and projects Jan has been involved with over the years, he will invariably mention the work with the very committed and spirited Amman Committee among the most satisfying.

SYDNEY, AUSTRALIA 2007

The study area: Sydney city center. Plan in scale 1:50.000

Sydney is a fine city for the Olympic Games, international summits, and waterfront promenades. But, the quality offered to people using the city center has, for many years, not been something to write home about. This was the background for Gehl Architects being asked for assistance in 2006.

In 2007, Jan and Gehl Architects were invited to undertake a benchmark survey of the downtown area of Sydney, Australia.[53] The survey was intended to be part of an ambitious long-term strategic vision for the city, Sustainable Sydney 2030.

The survey found that outside of the city's picturesque natural landscape and the famous waterfront areas, the city was largely dominated by car traffic, and as a result, treated pedestrians and public life very poorly. Effectively the city center was cut off from many of its major assets by streets and traffic, particularly an intersecting freeway and a bulky rail station between the city center and the harbor at Circular Quay. Despite the fact that 90 percent of all daily travel in the city involved walking, the city's streets did not do much at all to accommodate pedestrians. The survey determined that, overall, the city needed a much more people-oriented approach to planning and design.

The City of Sydney responded to the recommendations in the study by committing to pedestrianize the main thoroughfare of George Street, replace buses with a light rail, and introduce a city-wide bicycle strategy. The George Street pedestrianization was

The City of Sydney has a dedicated strategy for addressing the climate challenge: Sydney is committed to going green.

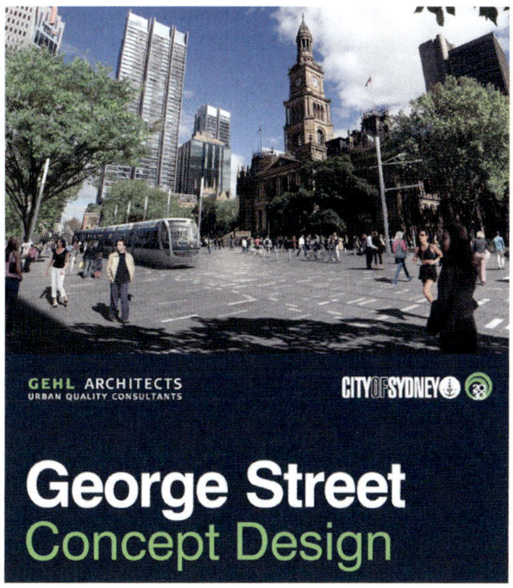

For many years, George Street (the main street) has been completely dominated by traffic, noise, and pollution. Transforming this main spine of the city into a pedestrian and light rail street was started in 2016.

politically very difficult. The survey report and Jan's presence in many public meetings and in extensive coverage in the media was instrumental in securing that the plan could go forward.

The light rail line running up George Street will connect a major university to the harbor front at Circular Quay, running straight through the spine of the city, past many important parts of the city. As part of this project, a major section of the street will become pedestrianized, with other sections being redesigned as a boulevard with wide sidewalks providing more space for pedestrians and outdoor cafés and activities. Sydney was awarded a Lee Kuan Yew World Cities Prize Special Mention in 2016 for its commitment to sustainability in the transformation of the city center.

The improvements have gone beyond the city center, with the city government working with the state government to create a bicycle and pedestrian network that connects the city center to the surrounding areas through separated and shared pedestrian and bicycle ways.

JAN GEHL'S INFLUENCE ON SYDNEY

by Lord Mayor Clover Moore, City of Sydney, Australia

Jan Gehl's Public Space Public Life study was an integral part of Sustainable Sydney 2030, the City of Sydney's long-term strategic vision for the next 20 years and beyond.

Jan saw the city's many positive attributes, including a wonderful public foreshore, great landmarks such as the Opera House and Harbor Bridge, extensive parklands, and a distinctive topography; however, the heart of the city was congested with traffic, buses, and noise. Jan asked the question—what do you value more, your people or your cars?

Jan's vision was to make George Street the city's great connecting spine, a mass-transit mall linking the grand gateways at Circular Quay and Railway Square with light rail and generous space for pedestrians. It would be accentuated by three civic squares, at the Circular Quay, Town Hall, and Central Station.

Jan's work in Sydney helped us convince government and other significant players in Sydney of the importance of unlocking the full potential of the city center. He provided the City with a timely and comprehensive set of challenging and insightful ideas and recommendations that ranged from the strategic level to detail that contributed to Sustainable Sydney 2030.

Jan's Public Space Public Life study reinforced our thinking for the future and the importance of public life and outdoor leisure.

Jan is a great communicator, and his passion for his craft inspired many people to see that the quality of our city could be improved and its true potential unlocked as a liveable, pedestrian friendly, vibrant, and exciting city.

Sydney carefully informs its citizens about the strategies and the projects to reach the goals. "In this city, we shall walk and bike."

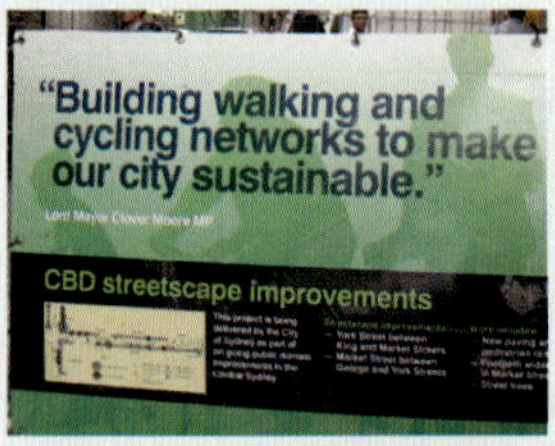

Inspecting the first stage of the King Street bike lanes. The Danish flag was proudly hanging over the scene. (The Danish Crown Prince met his Crown Princess Mary on this very corner.)

As part of the Green Sydney strategy, an ambitious program for new bike lanes is being rolled out.

Farewell, Sydney: One of the first undertakings in the improvement plan was to remove the monorail from the streets. It did not play a valuable transportation role, but was just a noisy ride with pylons disrupting local foot traffic.

NEW YORK, USA 2007–2013

Plan of Manhattan, south of Central Park ca 1:50.000

The Big Apple is globally significant and hugely influential for urbanists. For Jan, his role as advisor to the New York Department of Transportation has been especially significant. As he likes to sing (taking his cue from Frank Sinatra), "If you can make it there, you can make it anywhere".

In 2007, the New York City Department of Transportation, led by Commissioner Janette Sadik-Khan, hired Gehl Architects to conduct a Public Space Public Life survey. The aim of the survey was to provide the Department of Transportation with an increased understanding of how people used the city, to enable a better balance between transport modes and to inform a "wide range of ambitious programs" to enable the "renaissance" of the city's public spaces.[54]

The surveys and work undertaken in New York differ from the other cities in both the survey locations (including selected areas in the inner city as well as the outer city) and also in the outputs. The New York City

Many people are walking in New York, often on overcrowded sidewalks. Places for rest and enjoyment are few. There is room for improvement.

Just once in his lifetime has Jan's message been distributed in more than one million copies.

On a brief study tour to Copenhagen in June 2007, the New York Commissioners of Transportation and Planning, Janette Sadik-Kahn, and Amanda Burden had the opportunity to study the finer details of a people-oriented city strategy. This was the start of the involvement of Gehl Architects as advisors.

Department of Transportation produced their own report, "World Class Streets: Remaking New York City's Public Realm"[55] presenting key aspects of the collected data and an overview of their own public realm policies. This is different than Jan producing the report and then presenting it with recommendations to the city, but it embeds Jan's theory and approach.

The surveys found, unsurprisingly, that the city's many pedestrians were walking on overcrowded sidewalks and that there were few places to sit and spend time. The public places in the city were rather few and often difficult to access and unwelcoming. The streets in New York were mainly places to get through quickly on the way to somewhere else.

The results of the surveys gave the New York City Department of Transportation the data and information it needed to identify areas where they could implement changes and also highlighted some possible quick wins. Already in 2008, the DOT began making changes throughout the city at a rapid pace.

The changes included widening sidewalks, creating new plazas (often out of road space or parking space), and simplifying the user spaces of the street for safety by clearly defining where people should walk, cycle, or drive. Many of the changes were trialed first through pilot projects, testing what worked and what did not.

As part of this transformation, the city undertook a series of temporary street projects, such as Summer Streets where streets, including lower Park Avenue in Manhattan, are closed on selected Sundays in August. During Summer Streets, people are invited to walk, bike and engage in other activities, such as dancing and doing all kinds of workouts, in the street.[56] In 2015, over 300,000 people participated in Summer Streets.[57]

The most visible changes to the city were the new plazas and the increase in cycling infrastructure. Between 2007 and 2009, the city added over 200 miles (some 300 kilometers) of cycle paths, including protected cycle lanes along Broadway and a number of avenues. The number of people commuting by bike doubled between 2007 and 2011. Rid-

> *Until a few years ago, our streets looked the same as they did fifty years ago. That's not good business, to not update something in fifty years! We're updating our streets to reflect the way people live now. And we're designing a city for people, not a city for vehicles.*[60]
> —Janette Sadik-Kahn

Before the new bicycle strategy for New York began in 2008, ironic posters like these produced by activist groups were pointing to the problems.

ership is continuing to rise at a steady rate, although not as fast as it did when the initial improvements were made. The city now has 524 miles of bike lanes per nyc.gov/dot (843 kilometers).[58]

From all the changes made since 2007, 11 times more space available for people compared to the situation before. This is an extraordinary achievement. The most dramatic and iconic of all the changes is in the pedestrianization of Broadway at Times Square as well as Herald Square, Madison Square, and Union Square, and the redevelopment of Broadway into a boulevard. Times Square, in the 2007 surveys, was found to have severe pedestrian overcrowding, with over 150,000 people walking through the space per day, on narrow sidewalks with absolutely impossible conditions for walking.

To make the space more people friendly, the DOT initiated a pilot project in May 2009 that closed Broadway to through traffic at Times Square between 42nd and 47th Streets. Findings from the initial phases of the new plaza showed that closing the area to cars resulted in a reduction in pedestrian injuries, a reduction in pollutants, and that traffic circulated more freely in the other streets and avenues in the area due to better traffic management. The neighboring commercial businesses also reported an increase in revenue. The transformation of some of the roadway into car-free spaces enabled an increase in sales of 14 percent for businesses fronting this area.[59]

The trial closure was made permanent in February 2010 with a permanent design to convert the area into a plaza by Norwegian architecture firm Snøhetta chosen in 2012 (to be completed in 2016).

Right: 9th Avenue before and after introduction of one of the first bicycle lanes built as part of the new strategy to create a bicycle-friendly New York. By 2014, a total of 524 miles of street bike lanes had been built in New York.

AILEY

TOSHIBA
TDK
CHEVROLET
Budweiser
Kodak
RESCUE ME
Bank of America
WELCOME
AMERICAN EAGLE OUTFITTERS
STORE CLOSING
YAHOO!
LAKEFRONT
ONLY

One of the most important changes to New York has been the introduction of 50 new car-free public spaces, not only in Manhattan but in all parts of the city. Most prominent among the new public spaces will be the squares created by closing Broadway to traffic in major intersections.

Previous page: Times Square, spring 2009. This page: Times Square, summer 2009. This transformation has been a great inspiration for many cities around the world. "If you can make it here, you can make it anywhere!"

JAN GEHL'S INFLUENCE ON NEW YORK

by Janette Sadik-Khan, Bloomberg Associates; Commissioner, New York City Department of Transportation, 2007–2013; author, *Streetfight: Handbook for an Urban Revolution.*

My first "Jan-ecdote" began when I first met Jan in Copenhagen in 2007, shortly after I was appointed New York City's transportation commissioner. Mayor Bloomberg's PlaNYC sustainability agenda gave me the mandate to improve New York's streets with new public space, better public transportation options, and bike lanes built at a rate never seen before in the city. When I visited Copenhagen and met Jan, we went on bike rides, and had long, coffee-fuelled conversations about urban design at his offices or sidewalk cafés. We sealed a great friendship that would have a huge influence on New York City. I started by measuring, studying, and eventually tailoring Copenhagen's bike lanes to our streets.

I think New Yorkers were skeptical about bike lanes, period, much less the Copenhagen-style, parking-protected paths that we started building just months after that visit. People objected: "We're not Copenhagen! Bike lanes won't work here." I thought about how Jan might describe these proposed changes, which really helped frame the debate. Once implemented, these changes seemed like common sense and quickly became part of the city streetscape. We ultimately built nearly 524 miles of street bike paths in the city and they've helped increase the safety of everybody on the streets and attract millions of new bike riders to our streets every year. Jan likes to remind me that we built more bike lanes in the six years I was commissioner than Copenhagen did in 50 years. I guess Copenhagen isn't New York!

I asked Jan to come to New York City to lead one of his famous public life surveys, which was an important first for the city. You have to be a kind of urban forensic investigator like Jan to diagnose a street and know how to address its issues. He studied not just how many cars drive on a street, but how many *people* use the street, whether walking, biking, or stopping, and how they interacted with the space. Jan's study showed us that our streets were out of balance. In Times Square, pedestrians had only 11% of the space to walk on, even though they are nearly 90% of the traffic passing through it every day. Most of the space was given over to cars. If you stopped on the sidewalk, you could get knocked over by the crowd. It was so bad that people were trading the safety of the sidewalk to walk in the street. With this deeper understanding, my team at the transportation department began redesigning streets and iconic spaces to better align them with the way that people used them.

From the moment that we closed Broadway in Times and Herald Squares, the spaces were reborn and people immediately occupied every available square inch, while traffic moved on surrounding streets as well as or better than it did before. This also improved the area's economy, which was dependent on the hundreds of thousands of people walking—and not the tens of thousands of cars that merely drove through the area. The quality of the space was better, inviting people to stop and inspiring them to view their streets differently. This was an incredible feat on New York City's mean streets, and Times Square's impact has reverberated around the world as proof that cities can be built for people.

Jan's way of looking at our streets really underscored the opportunities hidden from building to building, curb to curb—what I call the public space hidden in plain sight. The story of our streets rests with its people. The energy, economy, attractiveness, and safety of a street and how it works for people are as important as the underlying infrastructure itself. If you aren't talking about designing streets to tap into the power of its people, you aren't talking about what makes cities work. And you aren't speaking Jan's language.

Taking up a tradition pioneered in South America, New York has also introduced car-free streets on selected summer days. A number of streets and squares are closed to traffic and opened up for all kinds of human activities: promenading, running, dancing, playing, and peaceful bicycling. Above: A residential street in Brooklyn. Below: Park Avenue in Manhattan, given over to people activities as part of the Summer Streets program.

MOSCOW, RUSSIA 2012–2013

Plan showing central part of Moscow ca 1:50.000

In 2011, Anton Kulbachevsky, the City of Moscow's Minister for the Environment, heard Jan present at an Ecocity conference in Montreal. He invited Jan and Gehl Architects to come to Moscow to assist in improving the quality of the public spaces of the city. In 2012, Jan and his associates undertook a Public Space Public Life survey of the central city areas, focusing on the city within the Garden Ring and the area around the All-Russia Exhibition Center, looking at public life in both summer and winter.

The surveys, published in the study report "Moscow: Toward a Great City for People" (2013), found that while Moscow had many attractive elements, such as a compact center, wide boulevards, and many beautiful green spaces and heritage areas, the city was "drowning in cars." The potentially attractive banks of the rivers and canals were used for traffic and parking rather than for people, and many of the vital elements of the city were hard to get to by walking and hard to find. Very little pedestrian traffic was found except

Plan showing the central part of Moscow ca 1:50.000 After commissioning Gehl Architects as consultants in 2012, the City of Moscow published three of Jan Gehl's books in Russian. Photo from the publishing event shows, from left to right: Alexei Dobashin, Director of Krost; Anton Kulbashevsky, Minister for Environment in the Moscow Region; the author, and the Danish ambassador, Tom Risdahl Jensen, seemingly looking a bit worried.

Moscow was studied in 2012 and found to be a city plagued with overwhelming traffic and parking issues while the visual environment suffered from excessive commercial advertising.

The absence of parking enforcement frequently made pedestrian crossings into obstacle courses.

Main street Tverskaya in December 2011. Cars are parked on the sidewalk leaving just one meter free for the pedestrians. The streetscape is grey, and commercial advertisements obstruct views.

Main street Tverskaya in June 2013. Instead of parked cars, there are benches and planters. The grey streetscape is gradually being greened; the ugly advertisements are gone, opening up views of the Kremlin in the distance. Jan has said that it was an almost miraculous turnaround.

concentrated around the subway stations, as a direct consequence of a very unpleasant pedestrian environment. People had almost stopped walking in the city and were using the subway for even short trips. Furthermore, many of the city's amenities were underutilized and had low visual quality.[61]

The space allocation in many roads and streets was inadequate for inviting people to walk, and many sidewalks contained obstacles and obstructions. For example, on the main street Tverskaya, there were as many as 30 obstacles per 100 meters. There were long waiting times for pedestrians at the intersections and few invitations to stay.

The recommendations in the report were to increase access to the river and green parks as well as to make radical improvements of pedestrian facilities in major areas.

Even while the survey was being conducted, some quite remarkable changes were happening in the city. The speed of transformation and improvement was absolutely breathtaking. Tverskaya, the main street,

By 2016, the City of Moscow had seen a remarkable transformation. Rules for parking had been introduced and were enforced. Traffic streets and parking places have become people streets and car-free squares. Left: Kuznetsky Most, 2013. Right Kuznetsky Most, 2016

had been nearly impossible to walk along in 2011 because of the continuous parking on the sidewalk. By 2013, the parking on the sidewalks had gone and instead benches, planters, and trees dominated the sidewalks. For Jan, the transformation was just short of miraculous. Even the advertisement boards, which used to clutter the views, were gone and the Kremlin was again visible at the end of the street.

Triumphal Square, in front of the important Mayakovskaya Metro station, used to be a square for traffic and parking. Now, there is no traffic and gentle swings are provided for enjoyment.

An important part of the city improvement program is the new wayfinding system.

Cleaning up the pedestrian crossings from parked cars and enforcing the new rules has improved conditions for walking considerably. Street scene then and now.

The two most important improvements found in Moscow by 2016: Strict parking rules have been put in place and are carefully enforced. A rather extensive bicycle infrastructure, complete with bike parking and bicycle street lights, has been introduced.

REFLECTIONS ON JAN GEHL

Excerpted from a letter by the Mayor of Moscow S. Sobyanin, on the Public Space Public Life survey and the collaboration with Jan Gehl and Gehl Architects.

Mayor of Moscow Sergey Sobyanin meeting with Jan Gehl in May 2012.

Currently, in the field of urbanization, the problem of creating high-quality environments is of great importance for cities all over the world. Comfortable social space is a source and a necessary condition of sustainable development of society and well-being of the present and future generations.

The cooperation between the Government of Moscow and Gehl Architects is an example of effective work on improving the quality of the urban environment. This can be called revolutionary because of both its scale and the content of concrete projects.

[...]

The Government of Moscow is undertaking complex measures in the field, including regulation of parking areas for cars; delimitation of territories for cars, cyclists and pedestrians; repair of pavement and pedestrian walkways; installation of small architectural forms; improved street lighting; creation of a convenient system of city navigation; additional planting of greenery; repair of building facades; dismantling of excess and illegal outdoor advertisement, and regulation of signboards. Pedestrian zones, bicycle paths, and bicycle parking areas are being created on the streets of Moscow.

Thank you, dear Mr. Gehl, for your devotion to the improvement of the quality of life for citizens and for your contribution to the development of safe, healthy, barrier-free, and comfortable environment for all types of citizens. This is exactly the way we intend Moscow to look.

The report "Moscow: Toward a Great City for People" from Gehl Architects was ready in the summer of 2013 and was put on public display in the streets of Moscow immediately upon translation.

PERTH, WEST AUSTRALIA, 1994, 2008 and revisit 2015

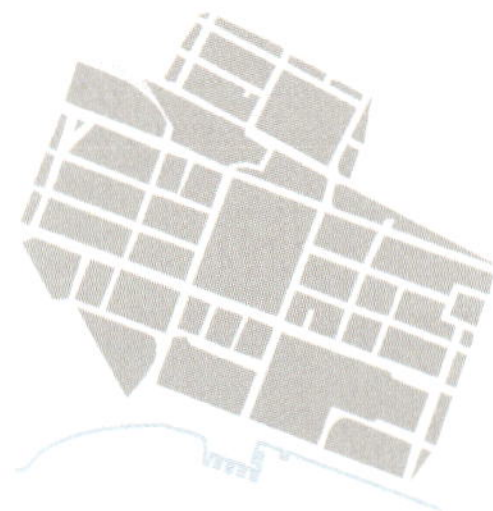

Study area 1993. Perth city center, ca 1:50.000 m^2

As mentioned earlier in the book, the 1994 Public Space Public Life survey in Perth carried out by Jan provided an "influential tool in guiding decision making" within the city center of Perth.[62] However, many of the specific recommendations for making Perth more people-friendly were quite challenging politically for the City and the state government who together had commissioned the report. The support of both was needed to implement the plan. Later, in 1993, matters were further complicated by a change of government.

The Perth study could have languished forever as a hidden and banished document had it not been for some strong lobbying from the NGO City Vision and some clever politicians who assured that the report was released for public discussion in 1994. The report received much positive publicity and public feedback. It seemed that Perth was ready for a change toward more humanistic urban thinking. The recommendations were accepted and began to be implemented in 1995.

In 2008, Jan and Gehl Architects were invited back to Perth to conduct a follow-up survey. It showed that there had been some progress since the 1993 survey in the humanizing of the city center. The surveys revealed that the city center had become less car-dominated and the city was greener and more welcoming. But, importantly, the surveys also pointed out that there was still much left to do before the city could shake its dull reputation.

The surveys showed a number of important areas in which the city could improve. These included the creation of a primary public space, a civic heart, and an increase in mixed use. The center of Perth was still predominantly mono-functional, focused on commercial and business activity. This limited the number of people using the city at night and on weekends. The Saturday pedestrian traffic was only 62 percent of the weekday pedestrian numbers, and night-time pedestrian count numbers had only increased by a few percent in the fifteen years between the surveys, even though the numbers of residents had increased. Furthermore, the surveys highlighted the absence of appropriate spaces for children, youth, and older people. The report, Jan's public lectures, and the media coverage provided the stimulus that the city needed, and reinforced the direction in which the city was moving. The City of Perth urban design team was emboldened by the report and dramatically changed the city over the course of the next five years.

One of the major accomplishments in Perth has been the increase in the number of residents in the central areas. From 7,800 in 1991, the number of residents reached 21,000 by 2015. Many of the new highrise buildings take great care to visually break up the building mass and secure a gentle landing in the pedestrian environment.

The program of widening the narrow sidewalks has been instrumental for enlarging the core city and for inviting people to utilize the sidewalks for a variety of activities.

THE PERTH STORY WAS JUST UNFOLDING

In February 2015, some 23 years after his first Public Space Public Life survey there, Jan returned to Perth. We were able to experience this exploration of the changes to the city along with Jan and some trusted veterans from the original Perth survey.

It was a profoundly moving experience for us to be with Jan as he saw first-hand some of the big changes that had occurred in the city, changes greatly inspired by his work.

Some of the changes were dramatic, such as the sinking of the railway to unite the two parts of the city that were separated by the railway infrastructure, and connecting the city and the river. Other changes were more subtle, such as the conversion of the numerous one-way streets to two ways and a general widening of sidewalks throughout the city, making room for benches, cafés, and street trees. The city is nearly finished with its two-way street program, slowing down traffic and enabling the widening of sidewalks throughout the city. The city has become enlivened in a way that was amazing even to those of us who have lived through the changes.

The redevelopment of the main square next to the central train station has been particularly impressive. The square features redesigned seating, a small stage, art work, and continuous pavement across the street that used to block the access to the station, but now, all on one level is linked to the train station. Importantly, the plaza has a water fountain, bringing water into the city, and signaling that Perth is a river city.

In September 2015, the Perth Central Business District was once again linked to the Swan River, when the massive earth works at Elizabeth Quay cut through the final barrier.

The most obvious symbol of change is the Perth Cultural Centre, which is strategically located in the center city. This center, once a rather bleak modernist monument with solitary cultural buildings standing freely in a sea of nothing, has undergone dramatic change

Turning a citywide system of one-way streets—made to accommodate more and faster car traffic—into a system with wider sidewalks and two-way traffic is a remarkable feat. In the initial phases, markers on street surfaces reminded people about the new challenges. The city even made a pamphlet, "Two Way Streets," telling about all the benefits of this change. An obvious result was that Perth became a much better city for people.

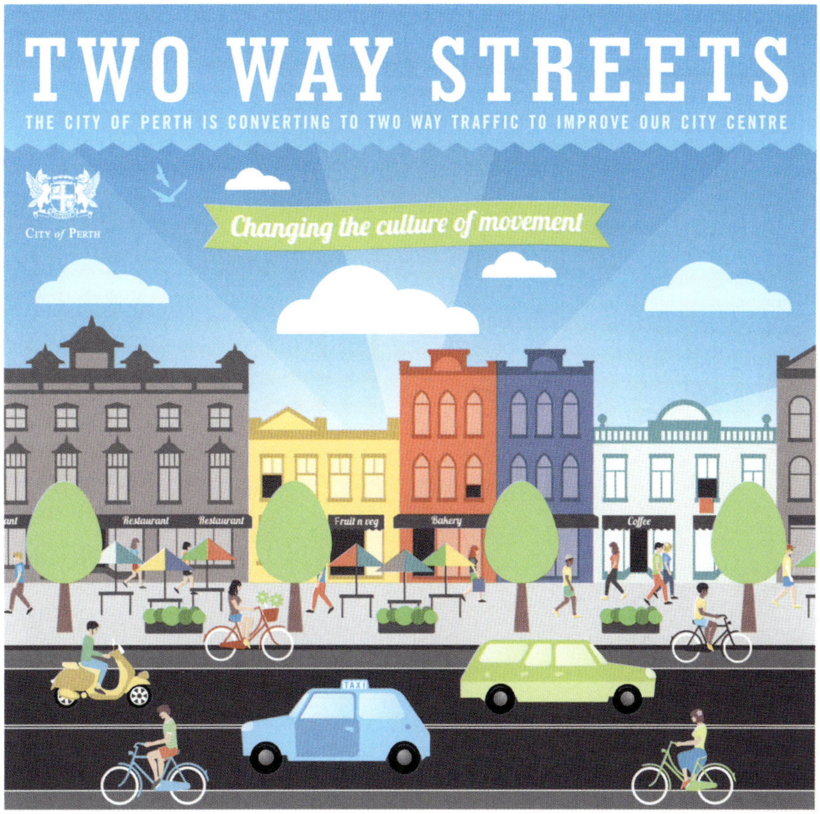

Murray Street in 1993 and 2015, now with two-way traffic, wider sidewalks, and street trees.

and is now a lively and interesting place. It is home to a greater number of culturally important institutions in Perth (see page x).

In the 1990s, the cultural center space was mostly deserted, except for people hurrying through. It was seen as scary, but it was the main connection between the northern and southern parts of the city center.

In 2004, the Metropolitan Redevelopment Authority created a vision to "infuse [the area] with creativity, culture and talent."[63] Jan, while not directly involved in the

The main square at Forrest Place was a somewhat sad place in 1993, dominated by footbridges to take people around the square and across to the railway station. In 2015, the bridges are gone, a good connection to the station is secured, and children of all ages have great fun with the water features.

In 1993, banners told people they were welcome, but the connection between city and railway station involved second-story footbridges and was indeed complicated. By 2015, all this is history and a wide pedestrian crossing connects trains and city.

redevelopment, had over the years prodded the locals to think creatively and boldly about the area and to see its potential. As with the other city examples, local champions and leadership are required for implementing innovative projects.

In 2014, Perth passed the 2 million population mark with 400,000 people arriving in just seven years. There is still a lot of suburban building going on, but the Perth city center population grew from about 7600 in 1991 to about 21,000 in 2015. Clearly, people now want to live in the city center as it has become reinvigorated (and, in part, their presence is helping to regenerate it), inspired to a high degree by Jan and his humanistic urban design. The future looks much more hopeful for Perth.

Aerial photo from 1993 showing the city at a respectful distance from its major attraction, the Swan River. Among the most important recommendations in the "Public Space Public Life in Perth" report from 1994 was to "walk" the city right down to the river. (Inset: Plan from the 1994 report.)

Below: Poster showing proposed design.

Below: The waterfront in 2015.

A miraculous revival. Both photos are taken from the same vantage point, in comparable weather conditions, and in the same season.
Top: Murray Street Mall photographed at 7:00 pm on an ordinary weekday in 1993.
Bottom: Murray Street Mall photographed at 7:00 pm on an ordinary weekday in 2015.

WORKING WITH JAN GEHL IN PERTH IN 1993

by Brett Wood Gush, Director Insight Urbanism

Did I hear correctly? Was my boss talking to his boss about Professor Jan Gehl doing a study on the City of Perth? In 1992, Professor Jan Gehl wasn't that well known in Australia, and he lived on the other side of the earth. However, he had astounded us with his presentation at a student architecture conference in Perth in 1985. Following his presentation, I had read his book *Life Between Buildings* and it changed the way I thought about architecture and cities.

I had heard correctly. In the days that followed, it was confirmed that Jan Gehl was being employed to undertake a public space study on the center of Perth.

Less than two months later, I was sitting alongside Jan as his lead project officer for the first Perth Public Space Public Life study. I was working with my hero and the City of Perth was paying me to be there! Jan was electric; people were drawn to the energy and excitement. Over several weeks, we built up a team and studied the city. We assessed the built environment and studied life in the city from dawn until late at night. Between focused research, we walked through the city sometimes with just a few trusted colleagues and at other times with the leaders and decision makers who held the ability to support or stop Jan's recommendations.

In the months after Jan went back to Copenhagen, I helped him put together the first draft of the Public Life and Public Space study. For a while, each step in the right direction took great commitment, and the strength of Jan's report became very clear. It showed how people walked around and used the city in a way that scientists and engineers were comfortable with; it talked about businesses, residents, and students in the way social planning and economists liked; it talked about place design in a way that architects and landscape architects could respond to, and it talked about the city as a place for people, culture, creativity, and inclusion in a way humanitarians expected. Most of all, it talked to all of us about something we all cared about, our city and our community. It was a simple report that managed great complexity, and so it became a constant presence in our minds and actions.

Jan's Public Space Public Life study has had a huge influence on several transformative projects. He encouraged us to bring the city and river together. That project is happening now, after some 20 years, and will restore the city to its traditional setting. Less visible, but as important, is his influence on protecting and enhancing streetscapes, promotion of alfresco cafés, revitalizing the city's laneways. His work provided the evidence and support for widening sidewalks out across the wide chasms of tar that once dominated the city, making room for seats, trees, and every kind of street life.

In 2010 Perth had done a great deal to design itself into being a better city. Still, it had not quite let go of over-managing how the city was used. Young and old called Perth "dullsville." They pointed to the success of Melbourne where, working with Jan, they seemed to have not only made the city more inviting but let the city become vibrant. Eventually, we too let go; rules were relaxed to let small bars, cafés, and festivals occupy the city.

Jan has been back many times since, invited to come back and update his report, update us, and share his passion with new leaders and practitioners.

Over nearly 25 years, I have come to know Professor Jan Gehl not just as a mentor and a friend but as an inspiration. I have presented on his methodology at countless seminars, looking to inspire other people as he has inspired me. Many of his best lessons, though, can't be shared at a conference. His commitment is to sharing his knowledge one-on-one with anyone, listening to people's views, finding the common ground, looking for a city's unique strengths, and tailoring his recommendations to its people. Above all, there is the consistency of his message. It does not change to suit the popular ideas of the moment but is aimed toward an enduring, timeless liveability.

GROWING PUBLIC LIFE IN JAPANESE CITIES

by Toshio Kitahara, Professor Emeritus, Chiba University

I first became acquainted with Jan Gehl through *Life Between Buildings*.

In the 1980s, Japanese cities were booming and their public spaces had been well developed physically. But unfortunately, most of them were lifeless. While there were many people on the street, they were merely walking from one point to another. What can I do to make the most of public spaces? That is when I met his book.

Gehl explained the relationship between public spaces and public life clearly, with many vivid examples. I learned much from him about how to stimulate public life in our public spaces.

In those days, the use of streets in Japan was restricted to the traffic by law. Then in 1997, I made an experimental demonstration to show how public life makes a street lively collaborating with Gehl. He and his students set up a Danish-style Copenhagen Square with a sidewalk café in downtown Nagoya. And Japanese teachers and students designed an up-to-date version of our traditional market stalls, right next to the square. Though those projects were small and temporary, they made a deep impression on people that life on the street was crucially important to the quality of the city.

In the next step, I imported a public life project into my university's hometown, Chiba, in 2000. It was a Parasol Gallery where people displayed their handmade crafts and paintings, and played music on a sidewalk of the main street. It drew a large audience and has become an annual autumn event operated by volunteer citizens.

In the last two decades, the Japanese government has changed its public space policy drastically and made new guidelines to promote various uses of public spaces. Public life is now growing in many public spaces in our cities.

The Parasol Gallery in the city of Chiba is one of several projects developed in order to promote public life in Japanese cities.

In 1997, Jan Gehl and a group of students from the Urban Design Department in Copenhagen were invited to Japan to participate in a project demonstrating how public life could bring life to a city district in Nagoya. The team created a "Copenhagen Square" complete with café furniture, Carlsberg parasols, as well as benches and city bikes from the city of Copenhagen. Street entertainment every evening was part of the program, which lasted for a week and was a great success—maybe partly because of the free (Danish) beer sponsored by Carlsberg.

A&B Architektura & Biznes
Jan GEHL
w Krakowie
SPOTKANIE 21-X-2014
nowohuckie
centrum
kultury

7

GOING FORWARD

GOING FORWARD

"To bring about the process of cultural change, the Gehl philosophy cannot be an occasional afterthought but a constant reference point to a whole range of decisions made about the city spaces." [64]
—M. Robinson, 2004

In the twenty-first century, many cities around the world began to improve the quality of their pedestrian infrastructure and public spaces. Some of these changes were part of a larger focus on sustainability and the commitment of cities to reduce their environmental footprint. Within planning, an increased focus had also begun on human health and the impact of planning and transportation policies on public health out of necessity.

How people used cities started to change and, in particular, it can be noted that there was a global reduction in automobile use and increasing demand for walkable, bikeable, transit-oriented communities.[65] The last 20 years have shown a return to the city by people seeking new jobs and using the opportunities found only in dense, diverse, walkable cities offering the meeting spaces so critical for creative interactions in the knowledge economy. The public space, coffee shops, and other "third places"[66] that encourage people to meet easily have become a competitive advantage.

Jan has spent the last fifty or so years putting people back into the architecture vocabulary and urban design agenda. Much of Jan's research has focused on the changing uses of public space caused by changing lifestyles and demographics, reinforcing the links between health and the built form as well as improved economic outcomes from better human qualities in urban space. Jan contends, "This period has seen a transition from a time when the quality of city space did not play much of a role in its use, to a new situation in which quality is a crucial parameter. In the past, people had to use the streets and squares of the city regardless of their condition."[67]

Jan, along with colleagues Lars Gemzøe, Sia Kirknaes, and Britt Sondergaard, started asking, "What is the purpose of the public realm in the 21st century? [...] What meaning and function does life in the public arena offer us today? What are the changing expectations for city space?"[68]

The walkable economy is inherently in Jan's approach to urban space. People today have greater mobility and increased indirect communication than in past decades. Further, as Jan and colleagues observe, "new roles for public space and public life are defined in situations where daily life for many people continues steadily to be more privatized...Meeting other people is no longer an automatic part of daily life."[69] Walkability is now being associated with the high productivity outcomes of the knowledge economy. Despite technology and demographic changes, much of the transferring of ideas and knowledge continues to take place through direct people-to-people interactions. Walking, and the vibrant public life that goes along with it, has been rediscovered as a powerful force in economic competitiveness as well as providing great health benefits. Walkable areas are being celebrated not just for the fun they bring to people's lives but as much for their contributions to livability, sustainability, and health.

During this period, there has also been an explosion of humanistic urban design (see table on next page). This shift to a more people-focused approach to design in architecture and planning in global cities has resulted in an increase in publications, organizations, and conferences focused on public space, walking, biking, and how people use cities. The current urban design movements of place making and tactical urbanism exemplify this shift. Increasingly, urban design theory is based on testing ideas by using temporary design measures within public

City of Lublin, Poland 2015: "Year of Jan Gehl"

2015 was declared "The Year of Jan Gehl" in the Polish city of Lublin. Local organizations, universities, NGOs, and the City joined forces to promote planning for a better people city. In October 2015, Jan visited in order to bless the good cause and he was most impressed seeing all the initiatives being undertaken. Rides on the "Jan Gehl City Bikes" as well as encouraging addresses to the many fans were part of a memorable visit.

BRIEF TIMELINE OF HUMANISTIC URBAN DESIGN

Pre 1960s

1944
José Luis Sert
The Human Scale in City Planning

1956
First Harvard Urban Design Conference

1956
Team 10 established

1957
University of Pennsylvania, civic design program

1958
William H. Whtye
The Exploding Metropolis

1959
Edward T. Hall
The Silent Language

1959
Congrès Internationaux d'Architecture Moderne (International Congress of Modern Architecture, CIAM) dissolves

1960s

Reaction to Modernism
Social upheaval, rights, environmental movements

1960
Environment-behavior studies
Kevin Lynch
The Image of the City

1961
Jane Jacobs
The Death and Life of Great American Cities

1961
Gordon Cullen
The Concise Townscape

University of California, Berkeley's Simulation of how people could view new projects (Peter Bosselmann)

1960
Harvard University Graduate School of Design and urban design program

1964
Appleyard, Kevin Lynch & J.R. Myer
The View from the Road

1966
Edward T. Hall
The Hidden Dimension

1969
Robert Sommer
Personal Space

1970s

Oil Embargo
Increasing concern about the environment

1970
William H. Whyte
Street Life Project

1971
Jan Gehl (1987 English)
Life Between Buildings

1972
Joint Centre for Urban Design at Oxford Brookes University

1975
Project for Public Spaces (PPS)

1975
Clare Cooper Marcus*
Easter Hill Village

1977
Amos Rapoport
Human Aspects of Urban Form

1977
Christopher Alexander et al.
A Pattern Language

1978
Urban Design Group

* Clare Cooper Marcus at the time of this work in 1975 was Clare C. Cooper. However, for consistency, she is referred to as Cooper Marcus throughout.

1980s

1980
William H. Whyte
Social Life of Small Urban Spaces

1981
Kevin Lynch
A Theory of Good City Form

1981
Donald Appleyard
Livable Streets

1982
Jonathan Barnett
Introduction to Urban Design

1985
Allan Jacobs
Looking at Cities

1987
Alexander et al.
A New Theory of Urban Design

1988
William H. Whyte
City: Rediscovering the Center

1986
Clare C. Marcus & Wendy Sarkissian
Housing as if People Mattered

1990s	2000s	2010s	2010s

1993
The Congress for the New Urbanism
Start of the Place Making theories

1993
Allan Jacobs
Great Streets

1998
Peter Bosselmann
Representation of Places

1993, 1998 (2nd ed.)
Clare C. Marcus & Carolyn Francis
People Places

1996
Jan Gehl & Lars Gemzøe
*Public Space Public Life—*Copenhagen, 1996

2000
Walk21 International walking conference start

2000
How to Turn a Place Around, Project for Public Spaces

2000
Jan Gehl & Lars Gemzøe
New City Spaces

Start of the human health (active travel) focus in urban design

Start of the 'Liveable cities' conferences and global rankings

2003
Matthew Carmona, Tim Heath Taner & Steve Tiesdell
Public Places Urban Spaces – The Dimension of Urban Design

2006
Jan Gehl
New City Life

2006
International Charter for Walking

2010
Jan Gehl
Cities for People

2010
Goldsmith & Elizabeth (Eds)
What We See: Advancing the Observations of Jane Jacobs

2013, 2014, 2015
The Future of Places Conferences

2012
Hans Karssenberg et al. (Eds), *The City at Eye Level*

2013
Jan Gehl & Birgitte Svarre
How to Study Public Life

2013
Reid Ewing & Otto Clemente
Measuring Urban Design: Metrics for Livable Places

2013
Urban Street Design Guide by National Association of City Transportation Officials – street design book focused on streets for people along with cars

2013
Victor Dover & John Massengale
Street Design: The Secret to Great Cities and Towns

2013
Charles Montgomery
Happy City: Transforming Our Lives Through Urban Design

2013
Jeff Speck
Walkable City: How Downtown Can Save America, One Step at a Time

2014
First Place Making master's degree (Urban Placemaking and Management M. S.; Pratt)

2015
Knights Foundation City Challenge

2015
United Nations adopt the Sustainable Development Goals, with a goal specifically on cities and public space

Start of the Tactical Urbanism movement

2015
Mike Lydon & Anthony Garcia
Tactical Urbanism: Short-term Action for Long-term Change

2016
United Nations Habitat III

2016
Annie Matan & Peter Newman
People Cities: The Life and Legacy of Jan Gehl

spaces to see how people use the space before making permanent changes.

We believe that one of the most powerful examples of Jan's influence on a city and a shift to planning for people rather than traffic flow is in the story of Perth. This book began with the depressing story of modernist Perth. After 23 years, a remarkable transformation has been achieved, inspired by the first Jan Gehl survey of the city. A 2016 newspaper article by two architects in Perth looking back on this era pointed to three significant people who helped bring about the change from "dullsville" to being an exciting city center, one of which was Jan Gehl. But like in all cities, there is so much more to do. The surface has just been scratched on the modernist monolith.

So what are some key ideas from Jan that can be held onto as we move forward?

Jan's primary goal has been to bring people to the table, to make people visible, to highlight the importance of lively people-oriented public space, and to bring a better balance between people and vehicles. People cities must remain at the top of the list for urban designers and other urban professionals and politicians.

How? Jan's philosophy has been to address this goal positively and systematically. Consistency has been his key. Observe the city carefully, collect data on how it is being used, and engage as many people as possible in moving toward a better way for people by providing quality public space for them to live their everyday lives. This is always going to be a political process as well as a professional design exercise, so communication must be central. The way in which Jan conveys his message has been critical to his success. Although his message is always consistent, he maintains that every telling of it needs to be fresh, that "you must put your soul into it every time, just like any actor."

The core of Jan's approach is his development of a pro-human and pro-urban theory. He has successfully furthered his ideas through the development of a quantitative system of measurement and a qualitative art, his ability to use urban design as a political force, and to provide hope to those wishing for a better city for people.

Is there a secret to Jan's success? While working globally, Jan has always been deeply rooted in his community. His family lives close; he is active in his neighborhood and steady in how he lives his life. He says, "All the time I have been flying close to the earth; I have always been part of the very ordinary life." This is clearly reflected in his theories and urban design philosophies—it is always about everyday people, their behavior and the ground floor of cities.

This simple formula of trying to make people-friendly architecture and cities, where designers actually look at, listen to, and learn from the everyday use of a city by ordinary people, has been Jan's secret and is part of his life and personality as much as it is part of his work.

It is important to emphasize that Jan is not anti-car; he is pro-people. To accommodate people, he unashamedly recommends incrementally taking away car parking, slowing down traffic, enhancing transit and bicycling (as seen through the Copenhagen example). This is always a hard balance, but Jan has provided a way to see how far the balance has gone and how much more it could go. In the end, it is the space reserved for cars that is needed for people space in cities.

It is possible to collect material in a way that enables design to follow the needs of people in the city—and then become the political ally of such ideas by highlighting imbalances within the system. As Jan states, most of the actual physical changes that have occurred within the cities where he has worked were

1 Company bike helmets for Gehl Architects, 2006.

2 Park Day in New York, a great one-day park created by PPS, 2013.

3 The Brussels Minister for Planning Pascal Smet presenting his "Jan Gehl" meeting room.

4 View from rear: People from Gehl Architects are expected to be in the fast lane.

5 Banner at the Architecture Biennale in Venice, 2012.

6 Czech fan club promoting "Mesta pro Lidi!"

7 Publishing Life Between Buildings *in Bangladesh, 2008.*

8 Poster, Louisiana in Venice, 2012.

9 Professor Renke He and poster, Chancha University, China, 1998.

10 Poster, Nuuk, Greenland, 2010.

11 Poster, Montevideo, Uruguay, 2015.

12 Ready to spread the word—now with the Kazahk edition, 2016.

Scrap book

1
2
3
4
GEHL ARCHITECTS
URBAN QUALITY CONSULTANTS
5
LOUISIANA c/o VENICE
LIFE BETWEEN BUILDINGS
GEHL ARCHITECTS
6
vaše CITY!
7
8
LOUISIANA c/o VENICE
LIFE BETWEEN BUILDINGS
GEHL ARCHITECTS
9
Dr. JA
10
Byer for mennesker
11
AN GEHL
N MONTEVIDEO
Jan Gehl
12

THE GLOBAL UPTAKE OF JAN GEHL'S IDEA

by Tom Nielsen, Professor, Urban and Landscape Planning, Aarhus School of Architecture, Denmark

Aarhus 1995: Jan Gehl and his ideas were not a hot topic at the Aarhus School of Architecture in Denmark at the start of the 1990s when I was a student. In these pre-internet years, we were dependent on the advice of our teachers, on visiting lecturers, on magazines and books in the small library. My teachers were deeply engaged in extending the discussion on aesthetics and form from the 1980s. The school was visited by practically all the influential post-structuralist architects displaying interesting fragments to insert into cities.

Fine . . . but also totally removed from the perspective of the users.

But then: At the end of a lecture series where different star architects were invited to talk about their cars (!), quite brilliantly, the organizer Svein Tønsager included a talk by Jan Gehl on cars and cities. Having taken a peek at *Life Between Buildings* at the library, I went over to listen. The largest auditorium of the school was almost empty. I think that five people in total, including Jan and the organizer, were present. Jan did a brilliant talk absolutely unaffected by the general lack of interest.

Fast forward to Sydney 2008: Being with Jan in Sydney in 2008, working with Jan on a major city improvement project for Gehl Architects, it was difficult not to think of the contrast to my first experience with him. Jan was talking about basically the same things as in Aarhus the decade before, but now backed by more evidence on the transformative potential of his ideas. And this time, he gave a talk that was not confined to students but to citizens from all over Sydney. The subject of the talk was the future of Sydney, and more than 1,000 Sydonians tried to find room in the hall, standing in the corridors and literally hanging on the lamps. The reception to Jan's presentation was overwhelming.

Back in Aarhus, October 2015: I am participating in a public debate on Aarhus's new traffic and mobility plan. Jan is not here, but Jan's thinking is very much present in the proposal and strategy presented by the city. Jan Gehl and his work are referred to several times during the night.

Twenty years after the discussion of cars and people in an almost empty auditorium, Jan now does not even have to be present to heavily influence the future of the city on the exact same issue.

There is still a need to spread the word: Munich, Germany, 2016.

not implemented by him. Rather, he provided recommendations, vision, direction, and, most importantly, the tools, the quantitative and qualitative information on the existing city life within the city, and the theory to understand its implications. These contributions empower local urban designers, city planners, politicians, and others to make the necessary changes to the physical environment to respond to the identified local human needs.

Possibly, Jan's greatest role (and that of his colleagues at the School of Architecture and Gehl Architects) "lies in the progression and substantiation of quantitative methods to study human interactions with the built environment and in enabling these people-focused studies to be politically recognized as a necessity in city design and planning."[70]

This data on public activity, and Jan's immense communication skills, empower local decision makers to enable their city to come to life. Jan is able to articulate the choices that can provide a city with a clear path to a better future. He is not simply describing the city; he is changing perceptions of it, using urban design as a political force. His ability to challenge the forces shaping each of the cities, pushing cities to change and to tackle the dominance of automobile-based design and development is a skill that all cities need.

In addition to this is the power of hope. Jan's approach offers hope to disenfranchised locals by vocalizing and documenting what people instinctively know is wrong in their city, but is not often understood or easily articulated. By providing visions of what works in other places, mostly small-scale, common-sense solutions begin to emerge.

WHAT IS NEXT?

"After more than 50 years of neglect of the human dimension, here at the beginning of the 21st century, we have an urgent need and growing willingness to once again create cities for people."[71] Jan Gehl, 2010.

Jan has committed much of his life to improving architecture and public spaces for people. He fought to establish the ideas, to create a design practice that could help cities improve, and dramatized it through his many beautiful books.

Looking forward, how can we continue to create people cities? Jan's approach has been shown to have great power, but there are still challenges to come for the next generation of urban designers, planners, and architects.

What can be done to improve the "people city" qualities of the immense urban growth still to come in Asia, Africa, and South America? Can they learn from Jan Gehl's legacy and not to copy our mistakes?

Many cities globally demonstrate and must live with the failures of modernism. We cannot tear everything down, and places are continuing to be built following traffic and modernist planning manuals. Jan's work has shown how dull, lifeless places can be brought back to life. We have seen this in our own experience. The softening of the Perth Cultural Centre through introducing small, human-scale elements into the space is a good example of this, or, as Jan would call it, "bringing the people-scale in by parachute." It attracts people to stay in areas that were previously out of scale with human activity. But the question remains how do we do this in the big-box, placeless suburban landscapes of many cities? Many cities have vast areas of car-based suburbs and soulless expanses of shopping centers. The next generation of architects and urban designers will need to find ways to regenerate these places, recreating them as small cities with concentrations of people and activities and with a focus on accessible planning and transit rather than

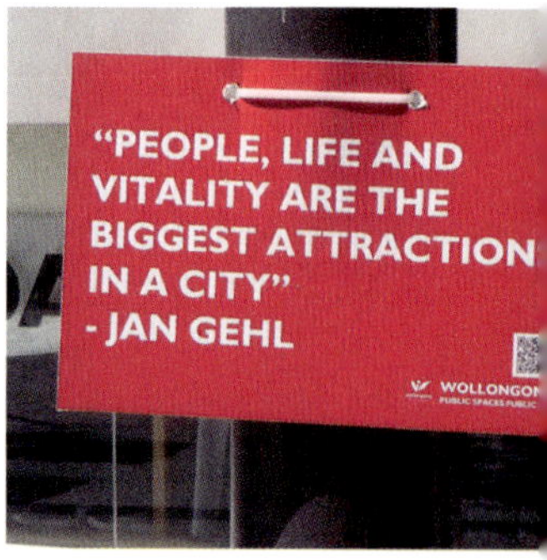

traffic engineering based on accommodating cars. Such centers can then become a focus for housing the growing number of people living in cities in thoughtful and appropriate ways, and in ways that create vital and lively public spaces.

When viewed like this, the task seems overwhelming—but then, how did it seem to Jan as he began working in the 1960s. There were almost no cities even thinking about how to address the issues of regenerating public life in public spaces. Jan's approach was to take one step at a time. He spent his professional career studying public life and how people use the public realm in cities in order to enable cities to be a little bit better tomorrow than they are today. This needs to be the goal going forward, but it is not without its challenges. Importantly, as Jan affirms, "I have never lost hope".

SUMMING UP

The legacy of Jan Gehl is that he provides us with hope. Every city has traffic issues that crowd out people from public spaces. Every city needs more provision of people-based public spaces. And they need the professional skill and political leadership to enable good options to be constantly envisioned and delivered. Jan has shown us how to do it in different cities across the globe. And the result has been extremely popular. As Jan says, "A good city is like a good party. People stay longer than really necessary because they are enjoying themselves."

As architects, urban designers, and planners, we have a huge responsibility to create cities where people can live healthy, productive, sustainable, active lives. For Jan, every day we must ask *"what would you like to use your life for?"*

Jan in Moscow, gently correcting Le Corbusier, 2016.

Writing on the wall. Town Hall, Alba Julia, Romania, 2016.

HOW TO STUDY PUBLIC LIFE
Jan Gehl & Birgitte Svarre
LEVEN TUSSEN HUIZEN
PUBLIC SPACES PUBLIC LIFE copenhagen
사람을 위한 도시
Jan Gehl
NEW CITY LIFE
Vita in città
Byer for mennesker
новые городские пространства
LIFE BETWEEN BUILDINGS
Using Public Space
Az élhető város
Jan Gehl
Cities for People
Linnad inimestele
Jan Gehl
Jan Gehl Cities for people
Život mezi budovami
La humanización del espacio urbano
LIVET MELLEM HUSENE
nye byrum
Jan Gehl & Lars Gemzøe
novos espaços urbanos
DET NYE BYRUM
LEBEN ZWISCHEN HÄUSERN
JAN GEHL & BIRGITTE SVARRE
nové městské prostory
new city spaces
CUỘC SỐNG GIỮA NHỮNG CÔNG TRÌNH KIẾN TRÚC
Des villes à échelle humaine

BIOGRAPHY
BIBLIOGRAPHY
ILLUSTRATIONS
NOTES

BIOGRAPHY

PERSONAL

1936	Born in Rønne, Denmark. 17 September
1961	Married Ingrid Gehl (née Mundt) 1963-1972 Environmental Psychologist 1973-2010 Child Psychologist and consultant
1962	Daughter Karen Julie Gehl (2016 Senior Doctor in Cancer Research)
1966	Daughter Anne Thora Gehl (2016 Team Director, International Media support)
1968	Son Jakob Gehl (2016 Economist, IT Consultant, Director Blue Solutions)

PROFESSIONAL

1951-1954	High School Sankt Jørgens Gymnasium, Copenhagen
1954-1960	School of Architecture, The Royal Danish Academy of Fine Arts, Copenhagen
1960	Graduated as architect
1959	Expedition to Greenland measuring old colonial buildings (The Danish National Museum)
1963	Expedition to Delphi, Greece for measuring and building archeological studies of the Delphi Sanctuary. (The French Archeological Institute in Athens)
1965	Studies of use of public spaces in Italy & Greece: (research grant from Ny Carlsberg Fondets Romer Legat)
1959-1961	Work as Architect in office of Viggo Møller Jensen and Tyge Arnfred
1961-1966	Work as Architect in office of Inger & Johannes Exner
1964-1990	Own office: Retstoring Medieval village churches in Denmark: Sejerø, Sjællands Odde, Sørbymagle, Ølstykke, Anisse, Skævinge, Snostrup, Gørløse, Værslev
1966-2006	Academic at the School of Architecture at the Royal Danish Academy of Fine Arts in Copenhagen
1966-1971	Research Scholar
1971-2003	Senior Lecturer
1976-1999	Head, Department of Urban Design
2003-2006	Professor and Director of the Center for Public Space Research
2000-2011	Founding Partner and Director, Gehl Architects APS (with Helle Søholt)
2011	Senior Advisor at Gehl Architects

VISITING PROFESSOR

1972-73 U. of Toronto, Canada
1976 U. of Melbourne, Canada
1977 U. of Waterloo, Canada
1978 U. of West Australia
1978 U. of Melbourne, Australia
1978 R.M.I.T., Melbourne
1978 School of Architecture, Oslo, Norway
1983 U. of California, Berkeley, USA
1983 U. of Guadalajara, Mexico
1985 U. of California, Berkeley, USA
1986 Tech. University, Dresden, DDR
1987 U. of Wroclaw, Poland
1990 U. of Calgary, Canada
1991 Univ. Of Gent, Antwerp and Diepenbeek, Belgium
1999 U. of Costa Rica, San José, Costa Rica
1999 Tech. University, Vilnius, Lithuania
2000 U. of Cape Town, South Africa
2000 U. of Yogjakarta, Indonesia
2000 Case Western Univ., Cleveland, USA
2003 U. of Costa Rica, San José, Costa Rica

MAJOR CITY IMPROVEMENT PROJECTS

From 1988, conducted by Jan Gehl

1988 Oslo, Norway
1988 Odense, Denmark
1990 Stockholm, Sweden
1994 Perth, West Australia
1994 Melbourne, Australia
1996 Copenhagen, Denmark
1998 Edinburgh, Scotland
1999 Aberdeen, Scotland

From 2000, conducted by Gehl Architects with Jan Gehl as project coordinator

2001 Drammen, Norway
2001 Riga, Latvia
2002 Adelaide, Australia
2002 Vejle, Denmark
2004 Wellington, New Zealand
2004 Zurich, Switzerland
2004 London, United Kingdom
2004 Melbourne, Australia
2005 Cape Town, South Africa
2006 Copenhagen, Denmark
2007 Rotterdam, Netherlands
2008 Perth, West Australia
2007 Sydney, Australia
2009 New York, USA
2009 Hobart, Australia
2013 Moscow, Russia

ACKNOWLEDGMENTS AND AWARDS

DECORATIONS

1967 Cavaliere dell´Ordine Al Merito della Republica Italiana

1967 Medaglia di Bronzo: Benemeriti della Scuola, della Cultura e dell'Arte, Italy

2011 Prince Eugen Medal for exemplary contributions to the Arts, Sweden

HONORARY DEGREES

1992 Doctor Honoris Causa, Heriot-Watt University, Edinburgh

2015 Doctor Honoris Causa, University of Toronto

2016 Doctor Honoris Causa, Dalhousie University, Halifax

HONORARY MEMBERSHIPS

2007 International Fellow, Royal Institute of British Architects

2008 Honorary Fellow, American Institute of Architects

2009 Honorary Fellow, Royal Architectural Institute of Canada

2010 Honorary Fellow, Planning Institute of Australia

2012 Honorary Fellow, Danish Association of Architects

2012 Honorary Fellow, Royal Incorporation of Architects in Scotland

2014 Honorary Fellow, Irish Planning Institute

EXHIBITIONS

2008 11th Architecture Biennale, Venice, Italy

2012 Louisiana, Museum for Modern Art, Denmark

2012 13th Architecture Biennale, Venice, Italy

2016 15th Architecture Biennale, Venice, Italy

NATIONAL AND INTERNATIONAL AWARDS

1993 Sir Patrick Abercrombie Prize – for exemplary contributions to town planning and territorial development. (The International Union of Architects)

1996 EDRA / Places Research Award, (for "Public Spaces-Public Life")

2000 Danish Guild of Pavers Prize

1999 Dalicarlika - Prize for public space planning, Sweden

2003 Australia Planning Award (with the City of Adelaide)

2005 Australia Urban Design Award (with the City of Melbourne)

2006 "EDRA / Places Research Award" (with the City of Melbourne)

2007 N.L.Høyen Medal for contributions on research and teaching concerning the arts. The Royal Danish Academy of Fine Arts

2009 The Commissioners Award for exceptional contribution to New York City streetscape and public realm

2009 Danish National Award for outstanding contributions to the arts and culture, (Annual allowance for lifetime)

2010 "Little Arne" award. Danish Association of Architects

2011 EDRA/Places Book Award (for "Cities for People")

2012 Medal of Honor, Danish Association of Architects

2013 C.F. Hansen Medal, The Royal Danish Academy of Fine Arts

2015 Global Award for Sustainable Architecture, Cité de l'Architecture, Paris

2015 Lewis Mumford Award, International Making Cities Livable

2016 Edmund N. Bacon Award, American Institute of Architects, Philadelphia

2016 Bertha & Carl Benz Award, City of Mannheim, Germany

BIBLIOGRAPHY

Mennesker i byer (People in Cities), 1966, with I. Gehl, published in *Arkitekten* 21/ 1966: 425–443. Language: Danish

Torve og pladser (Urban Squares), 1966, with I. Gehl, published in *Arkitekten* 16/ 1966: 317–329. Language: Danish

Fire italienske torve (Four Italian squares), 1966, with I. Gehl, published in *Arkitekten* 23/ 1966: 474–485. Language: Danish

Vore fædre i det høje! (Our fathers up above), 1967, published in *Havekunst* 48/1967: 136–143. Language: Danish

Mennesker til fods (People on Foot), 1968, published in *Arkiteken* 20/1968: 429–446. Language: Danish

En gennemgang af Albertslund (A walk through Albertslund), 1969, published in *Landskap* 2/1969: 33–39. Language: Danish

Livet mellem husene (Life Between Buildings: Using Public Space), 1971, published by *Arkitektens Forlag*, Copenhagen; Language: Danish (with English summary)

Studier i Venedig (Studies in Venice), 1972, With study group, published in *Arkitekten* 16/1972: 317–332. Language: Danish

Skandinaverne og vejret (The Scandinavians and the climate) 1976, published in *Landskap* 2/1976: 37–41. Language: Danish

The Interface between Public and Private Territories in Residential Areas, 1977 with F. Brack and S. Thornton, University of Melbourne, Australia

Studier i Burano (Studies in Burano), 1978, with study group., published in *Arkitekten* 18/1978. Language: Danish

Gågaderne der snublede… (The stumbling pedestrian streets), 1981, published in *Byggekunst* (Norway) 3/1981: 140–143. Language: Danish

The Residential Street Environment, 1980, published in *Built Environment* 1/1980: 51–61

Hvor by og bygning mødes (Where city and buildings meet!), 1982, with Å. Bundgaard & E. Skoven, published in *Arkitekten* 21/1982: 421–438. Language: Danish

Gågaderne i Danmark (Pedestrian streets in Denmark), 1984, with L.Brandt & H. Juul-Sørensen, published in *Arkitekten*, 3/1984: 50–63. Language: Danish

Soft Edges in residential streets, 1986, published in *Scandinavian Housing and Planning Research*, 3/1983

Byliv 1986 (Public Life 1986), 1987, published in *Arkitekten*, 12/1987: 285–300. Language: Danish

Life Between Buildings: Using Public Space (first version in English), 1987, Van Nostrand Reinhold, New York

Bedre byrum (Improving Urban Spaces), 1991, with L.Gemzøe, B. Grønlund & S. Holmgreen, Dansk Byplanlaboratorium Skrifserie n.40. Language: Danish

Jakten på den goda staden (The hunt for the good city), 1991, published in *Arkitektur* (Sweden) 9/1991: 28–33. Language: Swedish

Make one city and make it a good one, 1992, published in *Plan Canada* May 1992: 31–34

Nyhavn – 10 år efter (Nyhavn – 10 years later), 1993, published in *Arkitekten* 4/1992. Language: Danish

Fra Strøget til Strædet – 30 år med gågader i Danmark (From Strøget to Strædet – 30 years of pedestrian streets in Denmark), 1993, published in *Arkitekten* 11/1993. Language: Danish

Public Spaces Public Life—Copenhagen, 1996, 1996, with L. Gemzøe, The Danish Architectural Press, Copenhagen

Byens rum i Europa – og i Nordamerika, 1962–1996 (Public Spaces in Europe and in North America, 1962–1996) 1996, with L. Gemzøe, published in *Arkitektur DK*, 1/1996: 1–6. Language: Danish

Stadens form – stadens liv (City form – city life), 1997, in *Visioner av Kundskabsstaden*, Stadmiljørådet, Karlskrona, Sweden. Language: Swedish

"A Tribute to the Work of Jan Gehl and Lars Gemzøe," 1998, by Peter Bosselmann, University of California, Berkeley, USA, published in *PLACES*, Fall 1998

New City Spaces, 2000, with L. Gemzøe, The Danish Architectural Press, Copenhagen

Europas generobring (Reconquering Europe), 2002, in *Bykultur- et spørgsmål om stil*, Hovedstadens Forskønnelse, Copenhagen: 25–30

"Close Encounters with Buildings," 2004, with L. Kaefer & S. Reigstad, published in *Urban Design International* 2006. 11: 29–47 (originally published as "Nærkontakt med huse" in *Arkitekten* 9/2004: 6–21)

New City Life, 2006, with L. Gemzøe, S. Kirknæs, & B. Søndergaard, The Danish Architectural Press, Copenhagen

"Public spaces for a changing public life," 2007, published in *Open Space – People Space* in Topos, Calway, Germany

"Two Perspectives on Public Spaces," 2009, with A. Matan, published *in Building Research and Information*, 37(1), 106–109

Cities for People, 2010, Island Press, Washington D.C.

"For You Jane," 2010, published in Goldsmith & Elizabeth, *What We See: Advancing the Observations of Jane Jacobs*, New Village Press, Oakland

How to Study Public Life, 2013, with B. Svarre, Island Press, Washington D.C.

Documentary films

2000 *"Cities for People"(" Livet mellem husene")* Manuscript: Lars Mortensen & Jan Gehl, Director: Lars Mortensen. TV documentary, 56 min., co-production for the national TV channels in Denmark, Sweden, Norway, Finland, and Iceland. With English subtitles

2012 (Participated in) *"The Human Scale"* TV documentary. Director Andreas Dalsgaard

ILLUSTRATION CREDITS

Cover photo: Sandra Henningsson

Chapter photos:
Chapter 1, Page xii: *Street scene from Cordoba, Argentina*, Photo: Jan Gehl
Chapter 2, Page 8: *Photographing a Melbourne Lane*, Photo: Anna Esbjørn
Chapter 3, Page 26: *Welcoming banner in Korea 1992*. Photo: Jan Gehl
Chapter 4, Page 46: *Collage with Copenhagen street scene*. Photos: Lars Gemzøe
Chapter 5, Page 70: *Signing books in China in 2004*. Photo: Eric Messerscmidt
Chapter 6, Page 102: *Collage, Street studies in Australia*. Photos: Gehl Architects
Chapter 7, Page 150: *Book promotion bag, Kracow, Poland*. 2015. Photo: Jan Gehl

Photo credits:
Authors: Page viii, ix, xi bottom, 6 bottom left, 143 bottom, 144 bottom right, 145 bottom
Sandra Henningsson: Cover, page 3
City of Perth History Center Collection: Page 4 top, 6 top & bottom right
Public Space & Public Life, Perth 1994: Page 5, 6 top & bottom right
Other photographers: Page 34 bottom left
City of Copenhagen (former Stadsingeniørens kontor): Page 48 left
COBE Architects. Photo Rasmus Hjortshøj – COAST: Page 62
Alec S. Maclean, Landslides aerial photos: Page 65
POLFOTO: Page 67 bottom left
Nicolas T. Følsgaard: Page 67 top
Joachim Adrian/POLFOTO: Page 67
Eric Messerschmidt: Page 70
City of Sydney: Page 79, 122
Jens Rørbech: Page 83 left
Robert & Martina Sedlak: Page 91
Mikel Murga: Page 93, top
Kim Dirckinck-Holmfeld: Page 97
City of Melbourne: Page 100 right
Christine C. Finlay: Page 107 bottom
Grosvenor Estate, London: Page 117 middle & bottom
Thibah Consultants, Amman: Page 119 bottom
NGO Posters, New York: Page 126
DOT, Department of Transportation, City of New York: Page 127, 128, 129, 130
Toshio Kitahara, Chiba: Page 148 bottom
Astrid Eckert (photo © Astrid Eckert): Page 159

All other photos: Jan Gehl, Lars Gemzøe, and Gehl Architects

new city spaces
Jan Gehl & Lars Gemzøe
新城市空间
Jan Gehl
人性化的城市

NOTES

1 Jan Gehl personal communication. All Jan Gehl quotes without a reference are from personal conversations between Jan and the authors.

2 Jan Gehl, "Public Spaces and Public Life in Perth" (Report for the Government of Western Australia and the City of Perth. Perth, 1994), 9.

3 Ibid., v.

4 Ibid., 33

5 Charles Montgomery, *Happy City: Transforming Our Lives Through Urban Design* (New York: Farrar, Straus and Giroux, 2013), 147.

6 Ibid.

7 Jan Gehl and Ingrid Gehl, "Torve og pladser" ("Urban Squares"), *Arkitekten* 16 (1966): 317-329; Jan Gehl and Ingrid Gehl, "Mennesker i byer" ("People in Cities"), *Arkitekten* 21 (1966): 425-443.

8 Charles Montgomery, *Happy City: Transforming Our Lives Through Urban Design* (New York: Farrar, Straus and Giroux, 2013), 150.

9 The article "Mennesker til fods" was published in *Arkitekten* 20 (1968).

10 Jan Gehl, *Life Between Buildings: Using Public Space* (New York: Van Nostrand Reinhold, 1971, 1987 English Translation ed.), 47.

11 Ingrid Gehl, *Bo-miljø* (Københave: SBi-Report 71, 1971).

12 Quote from a public lecture presented by Amanda Burden, as reported in Katharine José (Producer). (2010, 17/09/10). "PlaNYC guru plays West Village: Gig is sold out", *Capital New York* (2010, 17 September), http://www.capitalnewyork.com.

13 Roberta Brandes Gratz, "Introduction: Authentic Urbanism and the Jane Jacobs Legacy" in *Urban Villages and the Making of Communities*, ed. Peter Neal , (London and New York: Spon Press, 2003), 17.

14 Jane Jacobs, *The Death and Life of Great American Cities* (New York: Random House, 1961, 2001 reprint ed.), 37.

15 Ibid., 110.

16 William Whyte, *The Social Life of Small Urban Spaces*, (Washington D.C.: The Conservation Foundation, 1980).

17 William Whyte, *City: Rediscovering the Center* (New York: Doubleday. 1988).

18 Edward Hall, *The Silent Language* (New York: Anchor Book Editions, 1973, 1959).

19 Edward Hall, *The Hidden Dimension* (New York: Doubleday, 1966).

20 Desmond Morris, *The Naked Ape: A Zoologist's Study of the Human Animal* (London: Jonathan Cape, 1967).

21 Jan Gehl and Birgitte Svarre, *How to Study Public Life* (Washington D.C.: Island Press, 2013), 60.

22 Jan Gehl et al. "The Interface Between Public and Private Territories in Residential

Areas," a study by students of architecture at Melbourne University under the supervision of Jan Gehl, School of Architecture, Royal Academy, Copenhagen, ed. Freda Brack and Simon Thornton.(University of Melbourne, Loma Print, North Melbourne, 1977).
23 Ibid.
24 Ibid., 5.
25 Ibid., 2.
26 Jan Gehl and Birgitte Svarre, *How to Study Public Life* (Washington D.C.: Island Press, 2013), 101.
27 Ibid.
28 Simon Thorton, architect and co-author of *Interface between Public and Private Territories in Residential Areas* (Melbourne University, 1976).
29 Peter Newman and Jeffrey Kenworthy, *Sustainability and Cities: Overcoming Automobile Dependence*, (Washington D.C.: Island Press, 1999).
30 Ibid.
31 Ibid., 155.
32 Center for Public Space Research, "Public Space – Public Life" (English Summary) (Copenhagen: School of Architecture, The Royal Danish Academy of Fine Arts, 2002), 49.
33 Ibid., 43.
34 Center for Public Space Research, "Public Space Public Life: Four Decades of Public Space Research at Kunstakademiets Arkitektskole." (Copenhagen: School of Architecture, The Royal Danish Academy of Fine Arts), 33.
35 Jan Gehl, *Life Between Buildings: Using Public Space*, English Translation ed., (New York: Van Nostrand Reinhold, 1987), 53.
36 Jan Gehl and Birgitte Svarre, *How to Study Public Life* (Washington D.C.: Island Press, 2013), 2.
37 Ibid.
38 Jan Gehl and Lars Gemzøe, *Public Spaces and Public Life*, (Copenhagen: The Danish Architectural Press, 1996), 11.
39 Ibid., 40.
40 Ibid., 59.
41 Jan Gehl, Lotte Johansen Kaefer and Solvejg Reigstad, *Close Encounters with Buildings* (Copenhagen: Center for Public Space Research/Realdania Research, Institute for Planning, School of Architecture, The Royal Danish Academy of Fine Arts, 2004). Originally published as "Naerkontakt med huse," *Arkitekten* 9 (2004). ed.).
42 Jan Gehl, Lars Gemzøe, Sia Kirknæs, and Britt Søndergaard, *New City Life* (K. Steenhard, Trans.), (Copenhagen: The Danish Architectural Press, 2006).
43 City of Copenhagen, "Metropolis for People: Visions and Goals for Urban Life in Copenhagen 2015" (Copenhagen: City of Copenhagen, 2009).

44 City of Copenhagen, "Urban Life Account - Trends In Copenhagen's Urban Life 2013," (Copenhagen: Technical and Environmental Administration, City of Copenhagen, 2013), http://kk.sites.itera.dk/apps/kk_pub2/pdf/1258_0B5eEF1cF5.pdf.

45 Athlyn Cathcart-Keays and Tim Warin, "Story of Cities #36: How Copenhagen Rejected 1960s Modernist 'Utopia'", *The Guardian*, http://www.theguardian.com/cities/2016/may/05/story-cities-copenhagen-denmark-modernist-utopia.

46 In 2015, it was ranked the world's most liveable city by the Economist Intelligence Unit's liveability survey for the fifth year in a row, receiving 97.5 points out of a possible 100 for health care, education, stability, culture and environment and infrastructure among 140 cities.

47 Jan Gehl, Birgitte Bundesen Svarre and Jeff Risom, "Cities for People", *Planning News*, 37, 4 (2011): 6–8.

48 Mitra Anderson-Oliver, "Cities For People: Jan Gehl," Assemble Papers, (2013), http://assemblepapers.com.au/2013/06/13/cities-for-people-jan-gehl/.

49 Robert Adams, "Reprogramming Cities for Increased Populations and Climate Change," in Esther Charlesworth and Robert Adams (ed) *The EcoEdge: Urgent Design Challenges in Building Sustainable Cities* (Oxon and New York: Routledge), 30–38.

50 Matthew Carmona, "The London Way: The Politics of London's Strategic Design," essay in David Littlefield (ed) *London (Re)Generation*, Architectural Design special issue ed. *London (Re)Generation* 82:1 (2012), 38–39.

51 Gehl Architects, "Toward a Fine City for People: Public Spaces and Public Life – London 2004," (Copenhagen: Gehl Architects, Report for Transport for London and Central London Partnership, 2004).

52 Ibid., 5.

53 Gehl Architects, "Public Space Public Life Sydney 2007," (Copenhagen: Gehl Architects, report prepared for the City of Sydney, 2007).

54 New York City Department of Transportation, "World Class Streets: Remaking New York City's Public Realm," (New York: New York City Department of Transportation, 2008). p. 3.

55 Ibid. And Peter Newman and Jeff Kenworthy, *The End of Automobile Dependence: How Cities are Moving Away from Car Based Planning* (Washington D.C.: Island Press, 2015).

56 New York's Summer Streets is modelled after Bogotá, Colombia's Ciclovia and Paris, France's Paris Plage. These programs are now found all over the world, including in Delhi, India.

57 The City of New York, Summer Streets, http://www.nyc.gov/html/dot/summerstreets/

html/home/home.shtml.
58 The City of New York, Bicycling in New York City (New York City Department of Health and Mental Hygiene, 2015), http://www.nyc.gov/html/doh/html/living/phys-bike.shtml.
59 New York City Department of Transportation, "Measuring the Street: New Metrics for 21st Century Streets" (New York: City of New York, 2012).
60 Janette Sadik-Khan as quoted in Lisa Taddeo, "The Brightest: 15 Geniuses Who Give Us Hope: Sadik-Khan," *Urban Reengineer Esquire* (2010).
61 Gehl Architects, "Moscow: Towards a Great City for People, Public Space Public Life 2013" (Copenhagen: Gehl Architects, 2013).
62 City of Perth, City of Perth Council Meeting Minutes, 16 September, 2008 (Perth: City of Perth, 2008), 44.
63 Metropolitan Redevelopment Authority, "MRA Central Perth Redevelopment Scheme" (Perth: MRA, 2012), 21, http://assets.mra.wa.gov.au/production/2661e75ff4441a3f09b1bb9f55e93612/central-perth-redevelopment-scheme.pdf.
64 M. Robinson, "Gehl Plans Left to Gather Dust," The Adelaide Review, August 2005.
65 Peter Newman and Jeff Kenworthy, *The End Of Automobile Dependence: How Cities Are Moving Beyond Car-Based Planning* (Washington D.C.: Island Press, 2015).
66 Ray Oldenburg, *The Great Good Place: Cafés, Coffee Shops, Community Centers, Beauty Parlors, General Stores, Bars, Hangouts, and How They Get You Through the Day* (New York: Paragon House, 1989).
67 Jan Gehl, "Public Spaces for a Changing Public Life" (Draft, personal papers, 2006).
68 Jan Gehl, Lars Gemzøe, Sia Kirknaes and Britt Sondergaard, "How to Revitalize a City," Project for Public Spaces, http://www.pps.org/reference/howtorevitalizeacity/.
69 Jan Gehl, Lars Gemzøe, Sia Kirknæs, and Britt Søndergaard, *New City Life* (K. Steenhard, Trans.), (Copenhagen: The Danish Architectural Press, 2006), 14.
70 Anne Matan, *Rediscovering Urban Design Through Walkability: An Assessment of the Contribution of Jan Gehl*, (Ph.D.), (Perth: Curtin University, 2011), 328.
71 Jan Gehl, *Cities for People* (Washington D.C.: Island Press, 2010), 29.

About Island Press

Since 1984, the nonprofit organization Island Press has been stimulating, shaping, and communicating ideas that are essential for solving environmental problems worldwide. With more than 1,000 titles in print and some 30 new releases each year, we are the nation's leading publisher on environmental issues. We identify innovative thinkers and emerging trends in the environmental field. We work with world-renowned experts and authors to develop cross-disciplinary solutions to environmental challenges.

Island Press designs and executes educational campaigns in conjunction with our authors to communicate their critical messages in print, in person, and online using the latest technologies, innovative programs, and the media. Our goal is to reach targeted audiences—scientists, policymakers, environmental advocates, urban planners, the media, and concerned citizens—with information that can be used to create the framework for long-term ecological health and human well-being.

Island Press gratefully acknowledges major support of our work by The Agua Fund, The Andrew W. Mellon Foundation, The Bobolink Foundation, The Curtis and Edith Munson Foundation, Forrest C. and Frances H. Lattner Foundation, The JPB Foundation, The Kresge Foundation, The Oram Foundation, Inc., The Overbrook Foundation, The S.D. Bechtel, Jr. Foundation, The Summit Charitable Foundation, Inc., and many other generous supporters.

Island Press | Board of Directors